Angel

Energy

Angel Energy

HOW TO HARNESS THE POWER OF ANGELS IN YOUR EVERYDAY LIFE

JOHN RANDOLPH PRICE

FAWCETT COLUMBINE • NEW YORK

A Fawcett Columbine Book
Published by Ballantine Books

Copyright © 1995 by John Randolph Price

All rights reserved under International and Pan-American
Copyright Conventions. Published in the United States by Ballantine
Books, a division of Random House, Inc., New York, and simultaneously
in Canada by Random House of Canada Limited, Toronto.

Library of Congress Catalog Card Number: 95-90164

ISBN: 0-449-90983-2

Text design by Holly Johnson

Cover design by Min Choi
Cover art by Susan Seddon Boulet (Brazilian, b. 1941),
Celestial Messenger, 1986. Oil pastel, ink, and pencil. © Susan Seddon Boulet.
Background photo © FPG, International.

Manufactured in the United States of America

To Jan

Contents

Acknowledgments

A special thanks to the angel within who suggested that I write this book and to the members of the Quartus Society worldwide, who responded to my call for angel experiences. While not all of the stories were used, I deeply appreciated your caring and sharing. My gratitude also to those who heard through other networks that I was working on this project and contributed their accounts of angel encounters; to Jan Price for her constant encouragement and inspiration; to my editor, Susan Randol, who expressed enthusiasm for the book before I wrote the first word; and to the staff at Fawcett Books, who have continued to help me write less and say more. Thank you all.

Angel
Energy

Introduction

The material for my previous book, *The Angels Within Us*,[1] began as a research project several years ago to help explain the unusual happenings that were taking place in our home. Now, I should tell you up front that I am not some mystical guru who delights in dazzling others with personal stories of phantom adventures. Most people—at least those who know me well—perceive me as a practical, down-to-earth sort of fellow not given to flights of fancy.

To give you a brief overview of my background, I grew up in the ranching and oil field country of south Texas, and in my adolescence the most important activities in life were dating, going to parties, and participating in sports. High school was completed without a single strange, unexplained happening.

My college years were also "normal"—I ran track, joined a fraternity, and changed majors five times until I finally decided on communications. After graduation, I spent twenty-five years in the pressure cooker of advertising, supervising the campaigns of several nationally known corporations and serving as president of two agencies in the seventies. Still no odd experiences, unless you consider the idiosyncrasies of a few weird clients.

Then, in 1981, my wife Jan and I formed the Quartus Foundation for Spiritual Research. That same year I wrote my first book, *The Superbeings*,[2] and a world of phenomena opened up. Strange lights began appearing in our bedroom at night, objects were moved, voices from out of nowhere were heard, and miraculous provisions in the form of money suddenly appeared in our bank account. There were other such occurrences, which Jan and I attributed to serendipity.

A particularly unnerving experience occurred one night in July 1985. While lying in bed, wide awake, I saw a large Being of Light walk through our bedroom door and move toward me. I was beyond frightened and pressed back against the headboard screaming, "No! I'm not ready yet!" The Being paused for a second, then turned and headed out the door.

Jan woke up and asked what was going on. I told her, then felt almost frozen—not with fear, but with a strong sense of having encountered something beyond the normal. Jan held me until my mind, emotions, and body returned to some degree of normalcy.

I started looking for answers, using meditation as a way to get in touch with a higher consciousness. After a period of time, I heard the words "archetypal plane" in my mind. I followed this up with extensive library research and eventually found those exact words in *The Secret Teachings of All Ages* by Manly P. Hall. He wrote: "The archetypal plane was considered synonymous with the intellect of the Triune Divinity. Within this divine, incorporeal, and eternal sphere are included . . . all that is, has been, or ever will be. Within the Kosmic Intellect all things spiritual or material exist as archetypes, or divine thoughtforms. . . ."[3]

In checking the dictionary I found *archetype* defined as "the original pattern, or model, from which all other things of the same kind are made; prototype." This meant that the original patterns of everything in the invisible and visible worlds exist in the omnipresent Mind of God, and thus within the energy field and mental sphere of each individual man and woman. Think about that for a moment. The model or prototype of everything "that is, has been, or ever will be" is *within us*; nothing is outside, all is a matter of consciousness.

Fascinated by the archetype idea, I was led to the works of astrologer-metaphysician Edwin C. Steinbrecher and the eminent psychologist Carl Jung. Steinbrecher wrote that "the archetypes are those energies which create and sustain our personal realities—aspects of God, if you will, that are experientially available to each and all of us."[4] And Jung taught that humanity's collective unconscious was a storehouse of primordial images, which he called archetypes, each having the power to affect human circumstances. He also believed that the Major Arcana of the Tarot were early representations of these archetypes.

Did an archetype from my consciousness walk into our room? Since everything is *in* consciousness, including the rooms of the house, it was certainly possible. But why did I yell that I wasn't ready yet? Probably because I wasn't ready to accept what this Light Being from the inner planes had to offer. (I learned much later that this was the Angel of Death and Rebirth who had come to help me give up the unredeemed characteristics of my personality—a dying of the old self in favor of a more spiritual consciousness—which was a frightful experience for the ego.)

By now I was beginning to wonder if archetypes and angels were not one and the same, that the substance of these messengers of God and guiding influences was intelligent energy in the universal subconscious that took form as living beings. Determined to understand their purpose, I turned to the Bible and found no less than eighty-two references to angels, "a race of beings of a spiritual nature . . . to aid and succor men on earth."[5]

After reading the accounts in the Bible, I was convinced that angels were beings of a spiritual nature living in the archetypal sphere of our energy fields—just beyond our conscious awareness. And how do they "aid and succor" us? I was reminded of a letter that I had received several years ago, one of many documenting the miracle-power that is continuously at work in our lives:

My sister and I were driving into town, and I was clipping along about 55 miles per hour and approaching a wide, sweeping curve. We were heavily engaged in conversation when all of a sudden an audible voice from some-where told me with some urgency to slow down. When I didn't slow imme-diately, the voice literally screamed ... "NOW" at me. I was so startled that I jerked my foot off the accelerator. Thank God! There around the curve stood a little boy about two years old. Had I not jerked my foot off the accelerator at that precise moment, I honestly believe I would have killed that little baby boy. As it was, I managed to stop about two feet from him. Can you imagine the feeling when you finally stop and here's this little blond fellow just smiling up a storm?

Can you accept the idea that an ancient archetype—an angel—residing in deep consciousness spoke to this woman, that a causal power within her was responsible for saving the child? The natural response would be to at-tribute this divine intervention to God. After all, God is Immanent, dwelling in all forms and "nearer than hands and feet." The Bible also tells us that God is "Father of us all, who is above all, and through all, and in all" (Eph. 4:6). And we know that our Divine Consciousness is God in expres-sion *as* us, as the very Reality of us.

Yet the masters, sages, and saints have understood for eons that this great Indwelling Identity remains in the absolute and does not control the world of effects: "The I AM is Spirit, and it cannot move directly on sub-stance. . . . It uses the spiritual faculties as its agents."[6] Furthermore, "Heal-ing does not come directly from God, Who knows His creations as perfectly whole. Yet healing is still of God, because it proceeds from His Voice and from His laws."[7]

As I was contemplating these ideas, it came to me that the guidance, the protection, the healing—all the aid, help, and relief—came from the *Light* radiating from the God-Self within, the intelligent conscious energy of the Spirit of God flowing into our minds and hearts. And I was reminded that this Shining into our personal consciousness has also been called the Holy (*Whole*) Spirit, the third aspect of divinity.

At that point in my meditation, it seemed that I stepped away and was looking back at myself, and I saw a brilliant Light, the Holy Spirit, entering my auric field and diversifying as distinct rays of radiant energy—as multiple streams of divine qualities representing the archetypes of all things spiritual or material. These were the angels, ready to provide everything needed in the journey through life. It was then that I knew I was involved in one of the most exciting research projects of my life.

In the *Condensed Bible Commentary* of the Authorized King James Version, we are told that the gifts from above "are direct gifts of the Holy Spirit. . . . The Holy Spirit implants them, and then develops them to stronger and higher degrees."[8] Ernest Holmes, the founder of Religious Science, wrote that the Holy Spirit is the "Servant of the Spirit. . . . the Holy Comforter, the Spirit of Truth, will make all things known to us, for He is with us and in us."[9] And Charles Fillmore, cofounder of the Unity movement, has written that "the Holy Spirit is the executive power . . . an emanation or 'breath' sent forth to do a divine work [as] the law of God in action."[10]

Djwhal Khul, the Tibetan master who provided the ancient wisdom for the books written by Alice A. Bailey, tells us that "the third aspect is, as you know, the creator aspect and the energy which produces the outer tangible plane of manifestation—the form side of life . . . it is with the third aspect and the third aspect alone that the creative process is concerned."[11]

In *A Course in Miracles*, we read that the Holy Spirit is "a Voice, for in that form He speaks God's Word to you. He seems to be a Guide through a far country, for you need that form of help. He seems to be whatever meets the needs you think you have."[12]

Out of the unity of Spirit comes the multiplicity of spiritual powers— twenty-two in all—each representing a voice, guide, teacher, revealer, corrector of mistakes, helper, producer, and distributor of those things necessary in our lives at this time.

Continuing research has revealed that these ancient archetypes predate all of the wisdom teachings and existed before any masters in physical form. In fact, most aspects of religion, philosophy, astrology, and metaphysics are directly or indirectly based on these causal powers living and working in each individual's energy field.

In our descent into the material density of the physical plane, we slowly began to lose our awareness of our spiritual identity. At the exact moment that the darkness appeared in personal consciousness, these powers of the Holy Spirit were sent forth to lead us back into the

Light and became permanent patterns of Universal Truth within each individualized energy field. The greatest of the powers, Unconditional Love and Freedom, came first as the awakening principle, but the "human" sense of mind could not readily accept it. So Love spawned other Shining Ones to assist us.

The Living Energy of Illusion and Reality was given to help us separate that which is false from that which is true in life. Creative Wisdom came forth to help us solve problems. The Angel of Abundance was sent to help us overcome a sense of scarcity. Every other aspect and condition of life on earth was considered, and the appropriate energy provided: Power and Authority, Spiritual Understanding, Loving Relationships, Victory and Triumph, Order and Harmony, Discernment, Spiritual Strength and Will, Patience and Acceptance, Courage and Perseverance, Imagination and Liberation, Truth and Enlightenment, and true Success.

We were also given the Energy to accept change and move into expansive cycles (the Angel of Cycles and Solutions), the Energy of surrender (Angel of Renunciation and Regeneration), the Power to help us overcome the ego (Angel of Death and Rebirth), the Energy of protection from the hypnotic pull of effects (Angel of Materiality and Temptation), the Inspiration to provide a greater service to the world (Angel of Service and Synthesis), and the Power to lift consciousness above miscreations into the realm of Cause (Angel of the Creative Word).

Here are the twenty-two angels within us:

The Angel of Unconditional Love and Freedom
The Angel of Illusion and Reality
The Angel of Creative Wisdom
The Angel of Abundance
The Angel of Power and Authority
The Angel of Spiritual Understanding
The Angel of Loving Relationships
The Angel of Victory and Triumph
The Angel of Order and Harmony
The Angel of Discernment
The Angel of Cycles and Solutions
The Angel of Spiritual Strength and Will
The Angel of Renunciation and Regeneration
The Angel of Death and Rebirth
The Angel of Patience and Acceptance
The Angel of Materiality and Temptation
The Angel of Courage and Perseverance
The Angel of Service and Synthesis
The Angel of Imagination and Liberation
The Angel of Truth and Enlightenment
The Angel of the Creative Word
The Angel of Success

A comprehensive list of the twenty-two angels is given in the appendix.

When we are of one accord with these spiritual faculties, our world becomes a reflection of the divine standard of all that is good, true, and beautiful. However, when there is friction in mind and heart and we are at odds with these powers, we find ourselves vulnerable to danger, conflict, scarcity, and less than ideal health. Doesn't it just make good sense to harmonize our relationships with these living energies within us?

These agents of Spirit anchor their powers just beyond our conscious level of awareness. From this base of operations they continuously project their energy to establish the reality that we must experience according to the state of our consciousness. Remember, the conditions in our lives are shaped through the trend of our thoughts and feelings, and these causal powers obey without question the exact vibration we are producing. If we are blocking their natural propensity to create and reveal glee and gladness, they will produce just what consciousness asks for—a certain amount of agony and anguish. If we repress an angel's quality of unconditional love, for example, we attract the opposite into our lives—animosity and resentment, which are projected back to us from other people.

Is this to punish us? No. The energies are simply subjective to our dominant trend of consciousness. Perhaps this was why the writers of the Bible warned us about "blasphemes against the Holy Spirit."

Everything in our individual worlds is an expression of either the freed (positive) or repressed (negative) energy of the twenty-two archetypes. As I discussed in *The Angels Within Us*, we free the angel energy by first forgiving ourselves for all mistakes and miscreations of the past. This action releases the energy of correction to do its healing work in our mind and emotions. The second step is to take a close and honest look at our negative personality characteristics—such as anger, arrogance, jealousy, and resentment—and the problems we may be experiencing in relationships, health, finances, etc. This self-analysis will help us see where we are blocking the angel energy. The third step in the process of freeing the angels is to release every flaw in consciousness and all the problems that are burdening us to the Spirit within. If there is a real willingness to let go and completely surrender everything to God, the ego is forced to withdraw its projections, and the natural process of life more abundant begins anew. The angel energy that we have freed and assimilated in consciousness is the energy force that performs the miracles for us—the sudden healing of an affliction, the unexpected manifestation of supply, the warning of impending danger, an intuitive flash that tells us to take a specific action, an inspiration that leads to greater fulfillment. When all twenty-two angel energies are working in harmony (freed from ego projection), we move into Cosmic Consciousness and experience the kingdom on earth.

The angels in unity represent an infinite treasure house that exists right now within our energy fields. It is the kingdom from which everything considered good and meaningful in life can be drawn. Our task is to learn to work with these agents of Spirit and free them to accomplish their glorious missions. This brings up the point of "making contact" with the angels.

Understand that we are in contact with each causal power at every moment. They are our energies and hear each word we say and feel every emotion we experience—and they will communicate with us if we can quiet the mind. This is why visible contact is important. The mind becomes focused, the inner ear attuned, and the meaningful dialogue begins.

To see the angel with the inner eye, you may at first have to use your imagination to create a mental picture. This triggers the energy of the materialization process, and the angel will take it from there, revealing to you the shape and form most suitable for your consciousness at this time. Communication with the angels begins with intuitive listening and feeling, which you translate into words. Deep mental impressions come later, and then one day you clearly hear the inner voice, which becomes stronger as the angels are freed from ego control.

The natural expression of the angels is *Truth*. If we deny the truth about ourselves and accept the illusion of limited, powerless, victimized humans, we repress the energy of the angels. But when we fully accept the eternal verities of life, our hold on the energy is released and the angels can begin to bring everything up to the divine standard.

Accordingly, our objectives are threefold in the chapters that follow: (1) to reinforce our understanding of the Truth of Being, (2) to bring the angels into balance by lifting the repression that we have forced on them, and (3) to witness the miracles that have happened in the lives of others who have embarked on such a journey of self-discovery.

For greater understanding in your personal odyssey, I suggest that you keep a journal on hand to record information and guidance received in dreams, during meditation, and from spontaneous transmissions from the angels that can occur at any time.

The unseen hands and inner voices are within us all, eager to comfort, guide, and assist us with every detail of life. They are just waiting for us to stop projecting our false images on their perception of reality.

It is time.

ONE

The Mighty Hands
of the Angels

Ralph Waldo Trine, a renowned metaphysician and author of "The Life Books" during the early part of this century, wrote

A Thousand unseen hands
Reach down to help you to their peace-crowned heights
And all the forces of the firmament
Shall fortify your strength.[1]

The unseen hands of the angels within are ever ready to lift us above points of explosive activity and fortify our strength to meet any situation.

The angel energies literally stream before us in rays of intense force operating at the speed of light, ever impacting the phenomenal world around us to maintain the law of harmony in our lives.

Interacting with expressed energy (what is happening or will happen in our personal experience), these agents of Spirit can override that which has been set in motion and literally change the outcome. Their reach is infinite, their power unlimited, and they are on constant guard, watching for vortexes of danger and potentially harmful pitfalls that may be along our path.

They may guide us with the voice of caution, but in many cases, the timing is so critical that words are dispensed with and those mighty hands immediately take over—to dematerialize form, steer an automobile, lift an immovable object, or erect an unseen barrier of seemingly solid substance to keep a child from falling into a raging river, as was the case of four-year-old Warren in Oregon. His father wrote:

I had been working with the angels since reading your book, and I feel that this was very important for what was to come later. I had taken my three children hiking in the woods, and we came upon this high bluff overlooking a fast-moving river. Holding each other's hands, we stepped a ways down the hill to get a better look when I began to slip. I tried to hold on to the kids, but Warren let go and was rolling toward the water. There is a sharp, steep drop-off just before the river and about ten feet above it, and that's where he was heading. I screamed, "Please, angels, now!" In a second or two he suddenly stopped rolling, even though the incline was quite steep. When I got down to him he said, "Daddy, I ran into a wall." I didn't under-

stand what he was talking about then, but I know now that angel hands formed a protective barrier for him.

Joy in Florida had two experiences with unseen hands.

In 1952 I got married and while coming back from Kentucky Thanksgiving weekend [my husband and I] were in an automobile accident. The car rolled front to end twice and over three times. I was thrown from the car, and looking up I saw the car coming down on me; then it was pushed back up on its side. I know my angels saved me.

In 1955 I was living in California with my husband, and my baby girl was four weeks old when we left to return to Kentucky. On the way there was another accident and I was thrown out of the car again. This time I felt a huge hand cradle me and my daughter and gently put us on the ground. Neither of us was hurt, even though we had been thrown about 100 feet from the car.

Here are other examples of the angels taking charge. Notice the similarities in the first three stories.

Richard was driving with his family on Bellaire Boulevard in Houston one winter evening, when he

signaled and stopped to make a right turn into a driveway. We all heard a crash of one car hitting another car. After the collision I pulled into the driveway and got out to help, and could not believe what I saw. The car behind me had rear-ended the car in front of me while I was still between them. My wife and children all agreed that the sound of the accident happened before I made the turn out of traffic.

Jean in Little Rock was riding as a passenger in an automobile when the following happened. The driver approached a green light at a busy intersection and proceeded through it just as another car ran the red light. Jean wrote:

A split second before the impending crash, we seemed to move into a higher vibrational state, and the two cars literally drove through each other—like walking through a wall. I can still see that car coming right at us, yet we and the cars were untouched.

And from Freda in British Columbia:

I was driving with a coworker when I ran a red light (I didn't see it). A pickup truck who had the green light bore down on us, not braking or swerving to avoid us, and traveling at top speed. I stepped on the gas in an attempt to get out of his path, but knew I couldn't. At that instant I thought I would die, and I prayed that my coworker be spared. Then a moment of unreality came over me, as if I weren't there, or was watching from a distance, and I could see that the truck went through the back half of my car. You might say that I misjudged the distance, but the front of the truck was at my door. I should have been killed and my passenger severely hurt. Neither of us can explain why we weren't smashed, but I can tell you that I said many thank-yous.

A letter from Gordon in Arizona tells of another miraculous event.

I was traveling on a state highway north from Tucson toward the little town of Catalina. It was a cold winter day in the desert, and the air was filled with a flurry of white flecks. Later I reduced my speed to about forty-

five miles per hour, on account of the poor visibility from what had become a heavy snowfall, and drove onto a bridge without thinking that it might have frozen over. It was. I realized it as soon as I saw the dim outline of an automobile that had jackknifed and stopped broadside across my lane. I slowly pumped the brakes but to no avail. I turned the steering wheel, but the icy road caused the back end to spin. Then I saw two figures standing at the edge of the railing in front of the stranded car.

As I approached the car in front of me, I had mental images of the front end of my car buckling from the impact. I gripped the steering wheel tightly, knowing that it would collapse and my chest would be driven forward. I had visions of being hurt and in a hospital. At the moment of impact, a flash of brilliance filled the view in front of me. Then a miracle. Despite the speed and the ice, the car stopped softly. It felt as if I had run into a giant block of foam rubber. And in my mind's eye I saw a magnificent winged being in front of my car, looking down at me. The angel stood some twenty feet high.

I managed to drive around the stranded automobile . . . and I burst into tears, more from the feelings I felt that emanated from the angel's presence than from a sense of gratitude for being saved—feelings of love, protection, truth, camaraderie, and eons of friendship. I shall never forget those moments.

And from Judy in Michigan:

I was walking home on a small town back street late in the afternoon. Two boys, about nine or ten years old, came out of the woods next to me *and started skateboarding down the street. All at once one of the skate-boards hit a crack in the street and stopped short—and the boy went sailing off, landing face down, sprawled across the middle of the street, not moving. Just then a truck going pretty fast for our neighborhood came around a curve and headed straight for the boy.*

I remember thinking, the driver is not slowing down; he's not turning his wheels to avoid the boy; he's coming straight at the boy. As if I were in slow motion, I raised my right knee to start running toward the boy and raised my hands to muffle what was starting to be a scream in my throat. The boy never made a move to lift himself up as the truck rumbled past me, yet in the blink of an eye he was out of the truck's way and walking over to retrieve his skateboard. The can of soda the boy had in his hands when he hit the bump was still rolling off to the side of the street. He soon caught up with his buddy and off they went.

The angels had to be there to snatch him up! I sometimes think how many lives would be so different today if that truck had hit the young boy.

How can an angel perform such magic? The same question was probably asked when Shadrach, Meshach, and Abednego walked out of the fire (Dan. 3:26–28), and the people watching "saw that the fire had not had any power over the bodies of these men; the hair of their heads was not singed, their mantles were not harmed, and no smell of fire had come upon them." This miracle was attributed to an angel of God, perhaps the Angel of Order and Harmony.

This particular angel controls the lines of force and rearranges the atomic configuration of forms: "She works with the form-building energy of all manifestation, seeking to transmute negative circumstances and to maintain the lines of force at their most harmonious level."[2] Thus, this angel is able to either lift us up above the perilous situation, change our vibratory rate to literally make us invisible to approaching danger, or erect an unseen barrier to protect us. As I have noted elsewhere, "Through the Light of Spirit radiating from within and moving into the third-dimensional plane, the pattern of the movements of electrons will be changed and the atomic structure of matter altered, including every 'force' on earth."[3]

I can understand this because I experienced such a phenomenon myself, although not quite as extraordinary as the other incidents described here. In 1992 I was involved in a rear-end collision involving five cars on a San Antonio freeway. I was the fifth car, heard the smashups behind me, and looked in my rearview mirror in time to see—and then feel—a car plow into me. We all pulled off the road, and for some reason, the man who started the chain reaction ran past all the other cars to where I was standing. I was looking at the back of my brand-new automobile and shaking my head. He said, "Are you all right?"

I replied, "Oh, yes—and there's not a dent or a scratch on my car, not even the dust on the bumper is disturbed. It's as though the collision never happened."

He shook my hand and said, "God is good," then ran back to the other drivers to inspect the extensive damage.

The angel had put me in a cocoon of light to act as a buffer. And yes, God *is* good.

A letter from June in Ohio shared another angel story.

During my time as a teacher of young children, I used the half-hour drive to school as a contemplative, quiet, prayerful time. One winter morning, while driving the scenic route in the country, I was lost in thought, forgetting the icy road as I sped along. All of a sudden my car began skidding. Although I knew not to slam on my brakes, I had to pump them because of the high speed I was going. As the car did a 360, I simply let go of my fear and said, "Angels, come close." At that moment I felt my car being pushed sideways across the road into a mass of beautiful, large, fluffy evergreen trees. They served as a cushion and brought the car to a halt. The caved-in driver's side of the car had $4,000 worth of damage, yet I had not a bruise mark, nor was I shaking. I felt serene and calm. I acknowledged my angels' presence and said, "Thank you, angels." No one could believe my condition—physically, mentally, and emotionally—when they saw the condition of the car.

You might think the story of the car ends here. Wrong! I had been telling my husband that I felt it was time to get rid of this car and buy a new one. I'd been feeling negatively about the car for some time, even before the accident. He said, "No, we'll repair it and it will be fine." Several months later, after repairing the car, I was driving in town and hit a large bump. I heard a strange noise, after which the steering became difficult. I knew some thing was wrong with the car, but I had one more stop to make before I drove the ten miles across the expressway to my husband's office.

I called upon my angels, saying, "Angels, come close. Please help me get to the office safely." After reaching the office, I took the car next door to be examined by the automotive service. The next day the mechanic told my husband he had no idea how I drove to his service station because the car had a broken tie-rod. Again, I thanked my angels. This time my husband agreed to sell the car.

George, a law enforcement officer, wrote:

It was a hot summer night in 1975 when I was driving my patrol car west on Center Ridge Road in Westlake, Ohio. I had a Pontiac Catalina that could do 120 miles per hour, but the vehicle had very poor brakes.

An auto passed me going east without lights at high speed. I turned around and gave hot pursuit. I did not put on my siren or red flasher. I was doing eighty when a black Buick with two older couples pulled out of the country club directly in front of me. I jammed on the brakes, but the Pontiac went into a skid sideways and just missed the Buick's rear bumper by a fraction of an inch. I lost control of the car and began spinning, missing telephone poles, fire hydrants, mailboxes. I sensed that I would die in a terrible wreck, yet all the time I was perfectly relaxed. Time became slow even though the auto was spinning at a fast rate. Everything seemed to be in slow motion.

The Pontiac finally came to a stop westbound by the curb. I was wet with sweat. I just sat there praying that my life was saved. I told myself that I would go to church that morning, and that I would go to church every morning to thank God. I knew someone else was steering my car. My hands had not been on the steering wheel. It had to be my guardian angel.

The Angel of Courage and Perseverance—the archetype Mars—does indeed have wonderfully strong hands. As a footnote, the police officer who wrote the above letter later became a minister.

The angels also work in what we may consider the ordinary affairs of daily living, ready to offer a helping hand whenever necessary, and frequently in disguise—as evidenced by this report from the same police officer.

We were on our way home from a vacation and had just passed Flagstaff, Arizona. We were pulling a small-tired trailer and realized that it could not make it to Ohio two thousand miles away. So we stopped in a remote section of the desert and decided to place the large wooden box on top of our Chevy. We also had two full-sized motorcycles on the trailer.

I was five eleven and weighed 214, and my stepson was a strong eleven-year-old. Together we could not even budge the box that was loaded with merchandise from Mexico. Suddenly, out of nowhere appeared a thin young man. He must have weighed all of 125 pounds. There were no autos in our view. He asked if he could help us. I smiled and told him of our problem. He said that he would place the heavy box on top of our auto, then lifted up the box like a feather and put it on top of the car and tied it down with a clothesline rope.

I turned to my wife and asked her if I could offer him at least five dollars, or give him a ride and take him to dinner. When I turned back to him, he had vanished. We were alone again in the desert. Surely he was a guardian angel.

Have you ever lost something and spent hours looking for it to no avail? Next time call on the angels for assistance. That's what Jo in New Hampshire did.

One sunny spring morning I was seated at the kitchen table engrossed in balancing the monthly checking account. My husband was leaving for a dental appointment, and I could hear him opening and closing drawers in the front hall desk. In keeping with the motto "A place for everything and everything in its place," it is our custom to drop our car and house keys in the right-hand drawer of the desk. After a few minutes my husband called out in a panicky voice that he couldn't find his keys and would be late for his appointment. After rummaging through every desk drawer, not once but several times without success, he gave up and set out to check the pockets of the clothes he had worn the previous day. Here again, he met with no success.

As I listened to this frenzied activity, I looked up at the Angel Calendar above my head and prayed, "Please, angels, help him find his keys!" By this time my husband had given up and decided to take my keys.

About five minutes after he left, I felt this urge to go into the front hall. The desktop was absolutely clear—except smackdab in the middle were his keys! Right then I felt the need to thank the angels.

When my husband returned home, I pointed to the desk and said, "Your keys have been found." Skeptically, he responded, "You placed them there after I left." I told him that I found them there after praying to the angels. He shook his head in disbelief. He remembered taking things out of several drawers in his search, then returning everything and leaving the desktop clear. As a matter of fact, upon exiting the house, he had to pass right by the desk and could not have overlooked seeing them in clear sight, had they been there at that moment.

We both marveled, but most of all, we thanked God and His angels for this manifestation.

Judy in Michigan, who wrote about the little boy and the truck, also had this to say:

I know that the angels are watching over me at all times, helping me through tricky situations, finding lost objects, putting me in the right place, and helping me say the right thing at the right time. I'm just getting to the point where I recognize the assistance of the angels, and I acknowledge their help and give thanks.

Sometimes I recognize the need for help in my life and I will ask out loud along the lines of "Angels, please help me." They know what I need and, without fail, the assistance arrives in short order. I may be overwhelmed at work with so many things that need to be done in a short period of time; I will ask for help and before I know it people are dropping by to offer their help, or time seems to readjust to fit the demands. Also, things just magically appear on my desk, things I thought I would have to search through files for. It is a great way to live—to recognize the help of angels.

Miracles will become everyday occurrences when we realize that the angels—our very own causal powers—are with us at every moment, turning heaven and earth to demonstrate the principle of harmony in our lives, thus fulfilling their purpose for being.

Laura Weaver, who works with us at the Quartus Foundation, agrees, and cautions us not to feel guilty about living a life with divine protection. She wrote:

I randomly opened the book, The Angels Within Us, *to the chapter on the Angel of Power and Authority. I read it and did the meditation at the close of the chapter, and suddenly I realized that all my life I have felt a helping hand in circumstances that most people would have considered difficult, if not impossible, to deal with. In some ways, I have even felt guilty about experiencing this sense of ease. As I poured out my gratitude to this Angel of Power and Authority, I felt his presence, and standing before me—as if a mirror image—I could feel and see a male figure dressed in shining armor and carrying a shield.*

We speak together often now, and he shares memories of our relationship when I was young, which I had blocked because of the feelings of guilt for always having a helping hand. Those feelings are gone now, and I've accepted my power.

Thank you, angel, for setting me straight and uniting us again.

We can condition consciousness to release the hidden hands of the angels through daily meditation. Here is one that I have used.

In the Mind of God there is only Infinite Perfection, and everything in my life is an expression of that Supreme Wholeness. Nothing comes to me except from the Father. Only that which is pure, good, and fulfilling can enter my world.

Divine Order reigns supreme in my life and affairs. All negative emotions are transmuted now, and I am joyous and free as I was created to be.

The Light of God surrounds me and I am at perfect peace. I rest in the green pastures and beside the still waters in total serenity.

Only the Activity of God is at work in my life, and God is Love. I let God's Love enfold me and care for me now.

The Power of God is my eternal shield. I am totally protected by Omnipotence, now and forever.

TWO

Inner Guidance from the Angels

"Guidance" may be thought of as counsel and advice—specific instructions coming forth from within to lead us in the right direction, to help us solve problems, and to help us stay out of trouble. Perhaps the author of Proverbs was thinking about the angels when he wrote, "Where there is no guidance, a people falls; but in an abundance of counselors there is safety" (Prov. 11:14).

Dr. Joseph Murphy, author, lecturer, and researcher of the world's major religions, has advised: "When you are perplexed, confused, and fearful, and wonder what decision to make, remember that you have an *inner guide* that will lead and direct you in all your ways, revealing to you the perfect plan, and showing you the way you should go. The secret of guidance or right action is to mentally devote yourself to the right answer until you find its response within you."[1]

The angels truly are guides, and they are responsive to all requests. As Murphy put it, "This response you will recognize as an inner feeling, an awareness, an overpowering hunch leading you to the right place at the right time, putting the right words into your mouth, and causing you to do the right thing in the right way."[2]

Many times Jan and I have asked for specific guidance when we were perplexed about a situation, and invariably the answer came. In 1979, when we were living in Houston, a man asked us to move to Austin and take over the management of his company. Something didn't feel quite right about the offer, so we took it into meditation. The inner voice said, "Go . . . it is time . . . everything will work out."

We accepted the satisfactory compensation package, including the payment of all moving expenses, and a few weeks later we were living in Austin. It didn't take long, however, to see that the firm was in dire financial straits, and that we had been brought in to perform some kind of a miracle. None occurred, and three months after we arrived, the doors were closed.

What about the guidance? In looking back, we felt that we were truly led to the right place at the right time, as we immediately formed our own communications company, which led to the writing of *The Superbeings*— and a more fulfilling life than ever before.

Kathryn in Michigan asked for and received specific guidance on the purchase of a new home. Here is her story.

I was blessed with the experience of attending the Angel Mystery School conducted by John and Jan Price in June of 1993. When I returned home I began working in earnest with my angels. I found a special kinship or bond with the Angel of Courage and Perseverance—the Mars archetype. He appeared as an energy body within beautiful purple flames. I often joined him in the flames in an embrace.

Now, to set the stage for what happened later, I had been wanting to move to another house for several years. I could see and feel it in meditation, but it just didn't materialize. In July, after attending the angel school, I spent endless hours driving in the country searching for "the" house, but nothing seemed right. Finally, I went in to see the Angel of Courage and Perseverance—my old buddy, Mars. I asked him about the perfect house for us, and he told me that the angels had been singing and dancing around my house just the evening before and having a glorious time. He said that I would find the house on August 7—told me exactly how much money to offer for it—and said that I would move into it on September 15, and that I would love it.

Well, I'll have to admit that I was a bit dubious, so I continued my search. Then, on August 7—just as the angel had predicted—the call came through. It was from a woman saying that someone she knew was thinking about selling a home, in an area so ideal that we hadn't even dared think about it. We looked at the house that night, and the energy surrounding it was just perfect. There wasn't a realtor involved yet, so my husband and I talked to the owner and said, "Yes! We love it!"

But how much to offer? I told my husband the whole angel story, including the money figure that Mars said to offer. My husband agreed, and the owner accepted. And yes, we moved in on September 15. What a joy!

What about those times when we don't seek an answer because we don't know the question? If we can't see a problem up ahead, it's not likely that we're consciously seeking a solution. That's when our intuition goes into high gear and we receive a flash of sudden insight from an angel to guard, guide, and inspire us to take, or not to take, a particular action. And we may verbalize it by saying, "I've changed my mind; that's not such a good idea after all"—"Something tells me we should take another route to reach our destination"—"My feeling says we shouldn't go to that party."

Of course, what we do with the information is strictly up to us. After all, we have free will, but I have found that when we dismiss the guidance as just our "imagination" and proceed as planned, we usually wish that we had listened.

There are five angels in particular who deal with preventing accidents, getting us through dangerous situations, prompting instinctive action, and helping us make intelligent decisions in an emergency. They are the Angel of Discernment, the Angel of Order and Harmony, the Angel of Courage and Perseverance, the Angel of Creative Wisdom, and the Angel of Illusion and Reality.

The angels can act alone, in pairs, or as a team. One experience I had in May 1994 reveals the combined power of all five.

Jan and I were preparing to visit a friend in La Paz, Mexico. Our bags were packed and our plane was scheduled to leave in a few hours, so we took a few minutes to meditate and tune into the angels.

Almost immediately I heard the words *"Do not go!"* I opened my eyes and smiled. Come on now, I thought, let's not get ridiculous. We're going to have a great time and everything's all set. Too late to change plans now.

Again, *"Change plans . . . do not go . . . listen!"*

I said, "If it's so terribly important that we cancel, then give me a sign." Now, this in itself was strange, because I can't remember asking for a "sign" before. I guess I wanted confirmation that the voice was more than just a subconscious desire to stay home and work on this book, which I was writing at the time.

Well, I got it—the sign, that is. Suddenly, something took me by the shoulders and started shaking me, and I found it almost impossible to get my breath. I was literally gasping, and it felt like a hundred-pound weight was pressing on my chest.

I stood up and walked around my study, and the sensation went away. Easing back into my chair, I quickly got centered and experienced that warm feeling of love and peace in and through me.

I asked, "What was that all about? Are we really supposed to stay home?"

"If you go, you will not come back."

That got my attention, and I went into the bedroom to tell Jan. She was getting ready to go to the post office. I said, "Something tells me that we ought not to go, that we should call off the trip. Maybe it's nothing." (Funny how we try to reason our way out of making a decision we know is right.)

She asked, "What are you feeling?"

"I don't know exactly." (I guess I wasn't ready to share with her the explicit warning I had received.)

"Well, you always try to follow your guidance, so don't stop now. Think about it, and I'll be back in a few minutes and we'll talk."

After she left, seeming a bit downcast, I turned within and said, "I don't want to disappoint Jan, so you just make the decision for us." (Even with all that had transpired in my study—the grave warnings and the physical sensations—it appears that I was still trying to find a way to catch that plane to Mexico.)

As soon as those words—"make the decision"—came out of my mouth, tears started streaming down my face, my body began to shake again, and I could not catch my breath. I heard the the inner voice say, *"You are not to take the trip . . . call the man and tell him that you are not coming."*

When Jan returned I was still a little emotional. I told her everything that I had heard from the inner voice, and she didn't hesitate. She went to the phone, dialed the number in La Paz, and told our friend that we weren't coming. She said to him, "I won't lie to you. The fact is that John was told very firmly that we are not to make the trip. Maybe we can do it at another time."

He understood and said, "If you find out why you were not supposed to come, please let me know."

Hanging up the phone, Jan suggested that we meditate together and see if we could pick up anything. We did, and during the meditation I was shown what seemed to be a vortex, a swirling black-green mass of tumultuous energy, and I became very cold. When I asked what it meant, the picture faded away. At the same time, Jan heard the word "boat."

Later that morning we went over to the Quartus office to tell our staff that we weren't going on the trip. Laura Weaver, who heads up the administrative section, said, "I knew that. Last night I dreamed that we took you to the airport. You and Jan boarded the plane, then immediately got off and went home."

That evening, Jack Cooper, the Quartus shipping manager, called to tell us that his wife, Julie, also had a dream the night before, which she remembered when Jack told her that we had canceled the trip. Julie got on the line, saying that she saw us all standing in a big room with lots of windows. We were looking out, and a man said, "We've got to get out of here, the water's rising." Julie said that at this point in her dream water was everywhere. Then she woke up.

We had not told our friend in La Paz any of this, and hadn't spoken with him since May 20. Four days later he telephoned to tell us that the word he received during meditation was that we canceled the trip because of danger on the water. He said that this was verified when he took his boat for a run, and out of a perfect sky came a sudden storm. Our friend made it safely back to port, but would have been much farther out on the Pacific if we had been with him at the time.

Thank you, angels.

The angels seem to be able to look around the corner, so to speak, and see dangerous situations in the making—as shown in this letter:

I was driving along a not too heavily trafficked street when I suddenly heard very loudly, "Pull off the road! Now!" There was such power in the voice that I never questioned for even one second where it originated or what I should do. I turned the wheel of the car quickly to the right and literally slid off the road, and as I did so a small red car whizzed past me in the oncoming lane, missing me by not more than an inch or two. Two days later an accident took place on that very spot—a head-on collision between two automobiles, one of which was a small red car, the driver of which was killed. A blind curve in the street prevented anyone from seeing the oncoming car.

A letter from J.C. in California also tells of a commanding voice:

It had been a hard week at work and I was heading down the L.A. 57 freeway, looking forward to my dinner date that evening, when I moved over to the off-ramp and slowed to a stop behind cars waiting to exit. Curiosity led me to glance over at a traffic officer issuing a citation on the freeway shoulder behind me. What I saw was a truck barreling down the freeway, swerving suddenly to take this same off-ramp.

"Lie down," came the command, and I pulled on the seat belt and turned to lie down across the front seat. I felt the truck slam into my car, felt

my car spinning around and crashing up against something, then stillness. I knew I was okay. I knew that I had been told what to do to save me.

The car was absolutely totaled. After the truck hit me, my car had spun around several times and was slammed into a larger truck in front of me. My car was demolished, except for the section I was in.

Angileen also heard a voice, and took the proper action:

It was with joyous expectation that I was headed for a spiritual center near Black Mountain, North Carolina. Suddenly, my reverie was interrupted by a loud voice shouting, "Get off the highway." I was right at an exit; an instant later I would have been beyond it. I obeyed the voice, and after a few miles I easily found a way back to the highway. It was deserted—no traffic going either way. I made excellent time and got to my destination only ten minutes later than planned. There I found concerned friends welcoming me. They had been watching a fifty-car, fog-related, chain-reaction accident on television—on the very highway I was driving— and wondering if I would make it through.

Guardian angels were certainly in that pocket of fog, too. Although it took six hours to clean up the mess, no one was injured! I was not the only one protected.

Oh, those wonderful, beautiful, protecting, guiding angels!

Linda in Minnesota heard the clear voice of an angel during a very confused time in her life. In December 1990 she and her husband adopted a baby girl, Megan.

When Megan was about two, we wanted another baby, and the praying started. We came close to adopting a boy in February 1993, but it fell through. Then nothing, until May 1994. Another miracle happened and a baby girl came into our lives. My husband and I were thrilled, not only for ourselves, but more so for Megan. Well, five days after baby Mary came into our lives, the birth mother changed her mind. We were heartbroken. Then in June 1994, another birth mother contacted us, saying she wanted us to adopt her baby, a boy. The baby was born on July 1, and we put the crib up and bought everything to get ready. The night before we were to go get our little Joey, the birth mother called and said that she had changed her mind. Why was this happening? I finally sought answers from the angels, and the day after I began working with my angel, I heard a loud and clear message: "Let go of the fear of losing Megan!" Now, I know that I would never have considered that on my own. I continued to ask for guidance, and a few days later another message came: "You are not responsible for Megan's happiness. God will and does take care of her and will give her what she needs."

I had been trying so hard to get her a sibling, because that's what I thought Megan needed to be happy. The messages have allowed me to release my obsession for a baby, and my mind is now at peace.

Let's take a closer look at preparing for inner guidance. The first step is to provide a communications channel for the angels by opening our intuitive nature. In one of my earlier works, *Empowerment*, I wrote about "the Pure Light of Intuition,"[3] and I believe it's worth repeating here. I had been contemplating "right decision–right action," and the message I received was later identified as a transmission from the Angel of Creative Wisdom.

The angel said,

> The Way is not shown through emotions but through the higher Mind, through the faculty of intuition. Feelings can be misleading for they are often reactions from the lower self. Even a sentimental emotion disguised as love can be an improper stimulus for action.
>
> A strong personal desire can also evoke an emotional response, which would be interpreted as a divine signal to move toward the goal, even while the higher Mind is suggesting a different plan of fulfillment. From this, one may perceive that mind rather than emotions represents the path of guidance. Yes, but the mind, too, may represent a pitfall, for mental reasoning and analytical thinking have only an affinity for past mental impressions, or the creation of new thought-forms cast out of recycled astral energy; in other words, the building of illusion out of illusion.
>
> To be instinctively guided along life's path, an individual must move above the emotions, above the rational mind, up to the knowing faculty—a point of Light emanating from the Higher Self. This Light is intuitional understanding. It is

illumination. It is ever-present radiating energy which leads
to omniscience in the latter days of the spiritual journey.

After pondering these ideas for a time, it seemed to me that the consciousness that is receptive to the clear light of intuition may be described as centered, detached, impersonal, quiet but alert, open to revelation, and focused in the now.

To experience your knowing faculty, come into balance and ask yourself what you intuitively believe about some point of concern in the phenomenal world. Then see the reality that is presented to your mind's eye, the clear vision that is expressed as an inner knowing. You may also wish to distinguish between illusion and reality through another exercise. Bring into mind a particular situation in which you find yourself, then ask the following questions and write the response:

1. What do I emotionally feel is the way to reconcile this situation?
2. What does my logical, reasoning mind tell me to do?
3. What do I intuitively know that I should do in this matter?

The objective of these questions is to solicit a response from your emotions, your thinking apparatus, and your intuitive nature. If done properly, the pure light of intuition—the angel energy—will offer the highest level of guidance.

Earlier I mentioned the five angels who work specifically in the area of guidance and protection. As we remove our ego projections from them, they are free to assist us with their clear voices and strong hands. The Angel of Creative Wisdom will be positively affected by raising our intuitive faculty to a higher vibration through the exercise above. She will continue to remind us—"Regardless of what your mind tells you, what does your intuition say?"

The Angel of Discernment will also work through our intuition to keep us on the straight-and-narrow path of high perception and deep discrimination. But first, we must overcome our feelings of insecurity around people and devote more time to contemplating the omnipotent Master Self within, the shining Sun who melts down all appearances of negativity in our world and "makes all things new."

The Angel of Order and Harmony expresses the energy of joy and serenity to keep us in balance, to inspire us, to keep us moving on higher spirals of life, and when necessary, to work in mysterious ways to protect us from the slings and arrows of this world. Her freedom comes when we give up the idea of conflict and sorrow and begin to express more gratitude for the good that is already present in our lives.

The Angel of Courage and Perseverance gives us flashes of clear vision—to see the Truth with the inner eye regardless of what is going on around us. He provides the power of boldness and determination to do the right thing at the right time and the energy of steadfastness to stick with it. Our role in releasing this angel from ego bondage is to overcome anger through forgiveness and to commit ourselves to a higher level of life and living.

The Angel of Illusion and Reality helps us to overcome mental fuzziness and to correct misinterpretations, and will gladly provide invaluable information regarding outer situations when we stop worrying about everything that could possibly happen to us or our loved ones. When we stop focusing on misfortune and concentrate on that which is good in life, the creative intelligence of this angel is released to show us the reality behind every illusion.

Here is a meditation to keep all these channels open.

I am poised and powerful in the Presence of God.

My emotional nature is quiet, my mind is still, and I am one with my All-Knowing Self.

Detached from this world, impersonal to illusion, I am totally open to the divine revelations from above.

From the radiance illuminating my mind I see only reality.

From the celestial note issuing forth from the highest realm of my being, I hear only harmony.

From the stream of crystal-clear essence pouring into my consciousness from on High, I know only the Truth.

From the pure light of intuition, I know the Way.

I am now able to take direct and correct action.

I know what to do, how to do it, and when.

I am a divine knower.

My knowingness now reveals ihe Plan and my part in it.
I watch. I listen. I wait.
I see. I hear. I know.
I now move forward to accomplish that which is mine
to do.

THREE

Healing the Past with the Help of the Angels

Life is based on the impersonal law of cause and effect. Every mental-emotional-physical action that we take is like a stone thrown in a pond. The ripples move out into infinity, producing corresponding effects. Accordingly, each *now* experience in life that is below the divine standard is nothing more than a scene from a play that we scripted at some point in the past appearing in the present moment. And that scene, which represents some form of emotional scarring—an obstruction to health, wealth, and happiness—may be repeated on our life-path unless we go back into the past and rewrite it.

I once gave a seminar on the use of retrospection to heal the past, a technique in which one relives a past experience and changes in mind what actually happened. This is not simply an exercise in remembering so that one could take a different course of action in the future. It is a correcting procedure to heal the past and actually change the future. I explained in my talk that when we go back into the past and review the experience, we can stop right there and rewrite the scene—we can literally edit the "videotape" and insert an episode that is gratifying and fulfilling. And when we change (in our minds) what happened in the experience, we are replacing all of the old negative patterns on the unconscious level relating to that experience. That which occurred before is no longer etched in consciousness to be replayed in recurring cycles.

With the help of the angels, Jan and I have done several life scans to "freeze-frame" events from the past that triggered emotional reactions in the form of fear, sorrow, guilt, embarrassment, and disappointment. The angels have shown us how to reconstruct each experience in its entirety, changing the dialogue, the actions taken, and the outcome. Through this modifying of history, this removing and replacing of activity in the memory bank, the whole chain of events from that point in the past to the present day was altered.

One woman at the seminar, who worked in the public school system in Houston, decided to test the procedure. Having devoted several months to establishing a relationship with her angels, she was ready to solicit their assistance in closing the doors to some of the more unpleasant yesterdays in her life. Here is her report.

This morning in meditation, I went in with my inner Guide and asked him to take me to the Angel of Imagination and Liberation. I wanted to work on a car accident from twenty years ago and rewrite history.

At first I saw nothing. Then I used the power of the Angel of the Creative Word and asked again for the Angel of Imagination to take form so that I could see her. And suddenly there she was . . . this female with denim short-shorts, a midriff peasant blouse, blond hair, and big loop earrings.

I laughed when I saw her and said, "You're certainly not what I expected."

She asked, "Why not?"

I said, "Well, you are pretty outrageous and funny."

She responded, "I'm your imagination, and I AM fun!"

I giggled and embraced her with love. Then I asked her to take me to the scene of the so-called accident. We went back to that time and place. She asked me to picture my car at that time—a '71 white Camaro with chamois-colored interior. I then saw that she was right there riding in the car with me, and I replayed, with her assistance, the whole scene.

I stopped at the railroad tracks, looked in my rearview mirror, and saw a man driving a blue VW hatchback. Instead of having the judgmental thoughts that I had back then, I sent him love and blessings. Then we went on through the intersection onto the freeway feeder road, where I saw an old man who was exiting the freeway so slowly that I had to come to a complete stop.

Instead of sending him my impatience and judgment, I sent him love and compassion. By this time I was sobbing. Then I realized that I had come in between the two cars so that the man in the VW would not hit the old man. At this point my angel-friend in the passenger seat said, "So, now do you want to rewrite the script?"

"Yes!" I answered. "I am ready!" Instead of a collision that caused a whiplash injury which had given me neck and shoulder pain for twenty years, we saw the man in the VW pull around to my right and pass me by— gently, easily, with no effort. It was done, and I really felt it strongly in my consciousness.

Then my angel asked me if it was all okay. I still had one last request . . . what about the old man? How do I know he is all right? So we replayed the end of the scene by seeing him continuing in the far left lane in front of me, and the blue VW passing him by also. I thanked my angel and hugged her.

A subsequent letter from the woman revealed that her neck and shoulder pain, along with other physical discomforts, had disappeared completely. Satisfied that retrospection with the angels can definitely be a life-changing experience, she decided to rewrite the past relating to her two previous marriages, as shown in this letter.

I wanted to heal any negative residue that could possibly cause obstructions in present/future relationships, so I called in the Angel of Imagination and Liberation again. She appeared as the woman with the blond hair and loop earrings. Chewing gum, she said, "Hi, honey."

I laughed and said, "You still look the same as the last time we met."

"Would you like for me to look some other way?"

"No," I answered. "I like you just the way you are. You're fun and you make me laugh and take myself lightheartedly. Let's get on with it."

I told her that I wanted to rewrite the past in my first marriage, and immediately I saw a scene with my first husband that had remained awful in my memory. I thought, Well, I sure need to heal that one. But with that thought I realized there were so many scenes to be rewritten in both marriages that this could take a long time. I wanted to do it more rapidly and efficiently, and I asked the angel if that was possible. She said yes.

It was then that I called the image of my first husband before me and took a good long look at him. I asked for that image to represent my entire relationship with him, to take a quantum leap of consciousness and heal the whole thing at once.

Suddenly, the awareness of all the wonderful aspects of our time together began coming in. I realized why I had brought him into my life, what I had learned from him, what he had learned from me, how it had been an initiation period for both of us. I thanked him and sent him all the love and forgiveness I possibly could. He received and returned them.

Then I asked my angel to show me my relationship with my second husband. He immediately appeared before me, and I saw all the wonderful times we had together—the love we had shared, the fun we had had, the beautiful child we had brought into this world. By this time, Venus, the Angel of Abundance, had joined us and was blessing this whole process. We also had the Angel of Loving Relationships with us.

As I let love heal all, I realized that it was possible to do it without re-

playing every so-called negative scene from our lives together. In fact, all of those scenes disappeared because they were illusion anyway. The only thing that was ever Real about either of those alliances was the love, the positive outcome, the lessons learned, and the life enjoyed and shared together.

As I recorded the experience in my journal, the following came through: *"Refocus, repicture, reframe those relationships and they become beautiful for what they were at the moment. They are the perfect building blocks, stepping-stones leading to the ideal relationship—the one you have with God, with your Master Self, which is now manifesting as your relationship with the new man. Thus you have the freedom to love from the context of your Higher Self. You have healed the astral sticky-stuff that would hold you back, or block your ability to love your Self and everyone even more creatively and spontaneously."*

I received the above letter in August 1993. In May 1994 this same woman wrote us again, saying that the new man in her life had given her a beautiful solitaire diamond engagement ring on May 7 and had asked her to be his wife. She added, "I'm writing to let you know that we're planning a wedding for July 30, and we absolutely cannot have it without you and Jan there."

We were there, and so were all the angels.

Linda in New Orleans also made a correction in her memory bank, an episode from her childhood. She asked the Angel of Loving Relationships to show her why she was having difficulty relating to men, and the angel took her back into time to see a moment of terrible verbal and physical abuse by her father when she was five. Her broken collarbone from that time had healed, but the emotional scar was still there. She wrote:

I knew that my relationship with my father had influenced my consciousness regarding other men, but I didn't know how all-pervading it was. With the help of the angel, I was able to not only forgive my father but to also look upon the incident with detachment. But the angel said that I shouldn't be satisfied with leaving it at that—that we should rewrite the incident. I began by eliminating my spilling the gasoline in the garage (near the water heater), which precipitated everything. I made it a bucket of water instead. And I had my father scolding me for my carelessness in a fatherly way, and not striking my body. I had to work on the changed scene with love for days, but finally it took. Now, instead of daily affirmations that the right man is attracted to me, I have the confidence that the two of us will find each other in the right way and at the right time. Also, I don't get nervous when I'm around men anymore, which to me means that a healing has taken place.

If you have been beating your head against the proverbial wall, trying to demonstrate right relations, a healthy body, prosperity, or simply greater peace of mind, something from your past may be blocking the flow of the natural process. You see, it is *natural* to enjoy ideal relationships, to be well and vibrant, to be prosperous, and to live life to the fullest. And when the past is healed, that's exactly what happens.

Regardless of your life experiences, there is an angel who can help you make the correction and get you back on the firm ground of the eternal Now. If past failures are haunting you, call in the Angel of Death and Rebirth or the Angel of Victory and Triumph. If fear still lingers over you because of something you did at another time, ask the Angel of Imagination and Liberation to help you dispel it. The Angel of Illusion and Reality is also good at this. To take care of the misqualified energy of guilt, see the Angel of the Creative Word. For feelings of injustice, either the Angel of Loving Relationships or the Angel of Order and Harmony will know exactly what to do. And a victim consciousness can certainly be changed by working with the Angel of Power and Authority and the Angel of Renunciation and Regeneration.

Make contact with the appropriate angel, then put your mind in the rewind mode and go back, slowly, until you find the scenario that is causing the problem. Forgive yourself and all concerned, and ask the angel to help you with the editing process. Together you are the scriptwriter, producer, and director. You are taking an old movie with the same characters, and you are changing some of the scenes to reflect only love, peace, joy, and understanding by all concerned, which will undoubtedly affect the ending.

It is important that you relive the new version of the experience with feeling. In the life-path, two scenarios cannot exist at the same time. It's like editing a tape. When you take something out, it is no longer there, and what you put back in, remains.

When Jan and I committed ourselves to the spiritual way of life—at least to what we understood "spiritual" to mean—things in our lives changed dramatically for the better. But as time went on we noticed a "cycle of return," a periodic reappearance of a particular kind of challenge. We would solve the problem each time it came around, but that old boomerang just kept coming back. That's when we decided to ask the angels to help us with a slow rewind, moving backwards and carefully scanning the pictures. We found the scar from an emotional wound that took place in the early 1970s, the result of certain business decisions with the ripple effect continuing through the years.

In reworking the script we followed the angels' suggestions and made entirely different decisions at that point in time, wrote new dialogue for all of the "actors," and produced each scene to reveal only love and harmony. And that particular boomerang hasn't been back since.

Jerry in Atlanta told me that after attending one of our workshops, he used the technique of retrospection quite successfully in forgiving a former employer. Jerry had been terminated from his job because of a poor performance rating and had directed his anger toward the vice president who had fired him. He wrote:

I would stay awake at night imagining how I could get my revenge, and the scenarios were becoming more violent as the weeks passed. I was out of work, and my despair over not finding a job added more fuel to the fire. I knew I had to have help, so I decided to attend your gathering. That was a turning point for me, because after I returned home I asked to be taken to the Angel of Imagination and Liberation, and together we edited the script.

I first saw myself as a better manager, more of a team player in the company, and more dedicated to my job. When it came time for my performance rating, I saw myself receiving only high marks. As far as the separation from the company, I wrote it as my doing—leaving to accept a higher position with another firm.

When everything rang true in my heart, I was satisfied that the past was changed. I was no longer hostile toward the man who let me go, nor did I feel any guilt over my previous attitude. You know what happened: I'm now working for my old company's major competitor at a better salary.

Amy in Los Angeles said that she was given some advice about the past by the Angel of Unconditional Love and Freedom.

I was told that my problem was nothing more than a cause-and-effect situation, that I caused the problem in the first place—then projected the blame onto my former husband. The angel said for me to forgive us both, even though my husband doesn't need forgiving, and when I do, the episode will stop producing ripples in my life. I'm still working on this.

To help Amy and others who may find themselves in the forgiveness predicament, play a game with me. Imagine that suddenly every activity of your life, including all personal relationships, was based only on the Now without any consideration whatsoever of the past. Imagine that all of what we consider the history of the human race, and of each individual, had been completely healed, that the law of cause and effect had been perfectly balanced from the beginning of time to now.

Would not our lives be different? Gone would be any reason to hate, to feel guilty, or to experience fear. There would not be any justification for personal conflict because we would not be judging the present on the basis of past experiences. By neutralizing the effects of personal karma, we could literally change the way we think about the past, which would immediately change the present moment and the future.

When we remember that everything is based on the law of a cause and effect, we see again that it is our consciousness that produces the undesirable experiences in life. Eventually we arrive at the conclusion that the outer world is only secondary to the inner world of consciousness, and our focus begins to change from without to within. We reverse our attention and begin to look for the crossed wires in our system, the faulty circuits that are limiting the Great Unlimited. And when the obstructions and impediments are removed through forgiveness of the past and a deeper awareness of our spiritual nature, the ego's projected effects begin to fade and are simultaneously replaced with higher impressions of a more substantial nature. Once this is done, the role of the past is simply to help us be aware of the purpose and function of everything; it becomes a resource for knowledge, rather than a source of retribution.

Confucius said, "Study the past if you would divine the future." We say, "Change the past and make the future divine."

I now let go of everything in the past that has caused me to think and feel less than I am in Truth—a whole and happy creation of God. I change my mind, and all that is no longer useful, loving, and joyful to remember is no more.

I forgive this world, and see it only as benevolent, for nothing can touch me but the activity of God, and God is love.

I forgive all, and feel no resentment toward anyone. If I am unable to do this, I call on the mighty Presence of my Holy Self to break the chains of ill will and animosity, for I choose to be free of the past.

I forgive myself, and surrender all guilt to the Living Fire within where it is consumed, and I no longer have to suffer any self-imposed punishment.

The pain of yesterday is gone forever. I no longer dwell in what does not contribute to peace and goodwill in life.

FOUR

Divine Assistance Is Always with Us

In researching the ancient archetypes, I made two important discoveries. First, when the twenty-two agents of cosmic law were given to us to help us find our way back into a consciousness of dominion, they became an integral part of our individualized energy fields. This means that these Living Energies must be recognized as our own innate spiritual powers. When we say *I*, we are identifying ourselves not only as a unit of consciousness but also as the qualities of divine force that make up that consciousness. Thus, *we* are the angels; the angels are *us*.

Second, while it is true that we can repress the energy of the angels through ego projection, it is also true that we can never subjugate all twenty-two powers at the same time. Regardless of our state of consciousness—and no matter how guilty we may be judging ourselves over errors in thought, word, and deed—at least one of the angels is always free to love and nourish us without judgment, or to work a miracle if necessary. Even the most closed minds can't completely shut out the Light. There is always a Holy Helper available when times seem darkest.

One man I know personally made this very clear to me. In one of his first letters to me (before we met in person), he said that he was an agnostic for most of his early adult life:

Yet from about age ten I knew and accepted the fact that I seemed to think and act differently from everyone else, and that I could not accept the angry, humanized god to which I was exposed in a fundamentalist religion. I believed that there was a power of some kind behind what I saw in the world, but I did not believe that it had any personal interest in humanity or me. Instead, I believed in myself. I seemed to know inside that I could do anything I chose to do, and in subsequent years I proved it. By worldly standards I was a success, both in my profession and in high offices of the federal government.

Later, however, this man experienced a serious leg injury, and the doctors told him that he would never walk again and would be in pain for the rest of his life. He lost his job and soon found himself in such a depth of depression that he decided to commit suicide. He wrote:

But before I could pull the trigger on my service revolver, the room flashed into brilliant light, the world turned rightside up and was beautiful, and I suddenly knew all there is to know, but could express none of it.

The greatest part of the whole experience was my clear awareness of a marvelous Being standing near my right foot. He was smiling and saying wonderful things to me, and he was with me (appearing visibly and speaking audibly) for about six months. We had many discussions in which I learned things about human destiny, as well as about my own functions and destiny. My life and attitudes were totally different.

Miracles spontaneously happened to me and around me. One of the greatest things was the sudden and complete rebuilding of my leg and ankle, which had been solidified by many bone grafts. The whole leg worked perfectly, and I have had no trouble with it since.

At first I could not express (not even in writing) any of what I had learned, and it was sixteen years before I was led to anyone having concepts similar to what I knew. So I developed my own methods for communing inside, and I used my knowing only to help or heal myself, because I did not then know that I could help anyone else.

Then, exactly sixteen years after my experience in the light, I had another similar experience. This time I was given a general idea of what I am to do, and the unobtrusive manner in which I am to work. Immediately after the second illumination I began to discover people with beliefs somewhat similar to mine. Then, a few months later, people began spontaneously coming to me with their troubles of every conceivable kind, both physical and otherwise, and most of them were helped. New cases came at an in-

creasing rate. They were mostly complete strangers, and they included even terminal cancer cases, which were cured, one instantaneously. I do not claim to have attained any special spiritual status, as I know that all people have the same potential that I have.

Jan and I finally met this delightful man, and the encounter can only be described as electric. The energy radiating from him was incredible, and from his eyes came forth the deepest love I have ever seen or felt. He also revealed a marvelous sense of humor, an unassuming manner, and a rare wisdom.

Who was the Being that appeared to this man? He didn't say, but a voice I heard when discussing this case with the angels said, *"It was the Angel of Truth and Enlightenment, the healing power of Spirit."* Of course! "The Angel of Truth and Enlightenment was known by the Egyptians as the archetype Ra, a being of sun representing the power that resurrects the soul, and to the Greeks he was known as Apollo, the god of the sun and light"[1]— the angel who "establishes a healing vibration in the physical body"[2]—the one who "lifts us up above the level of the problem and into the consciousness of the Shining Sun that radiates the fullness of the God-Self."[3]

Obviously, this angel had not been bound by ego projection and was free to respond in an emergency situation to prevent the suicide, to heal the man's leg, and to teach him "all there is to know."

Why this particular man? Perhaps because he believed in himself, not egotistically, but in a way that suggests he intuitively knew that he was more than what appeared in the mirror. Remember, he said that from about age ten he thought and acted differently from others—and as he told me later,

"The messages of Truth that I received during my experience did not seem strange. . . . I was most comfortable with the teachings." I have the feeling that this angel had been working with him for many years, waiting for the opportunity to reveal his true life plan.

I include his story here to remind us that we do not have to be in a state of spiritual illumination to have angelic assistance. Whenever we seem lost and confused because of our depressed state, there is always an unbound, unfettered angel right where we are, ready to help us find our way out of the shadows. We will discuss this further after we take a closer look at the meaning of the word *consciousness.*

Consciousness is a combination of our awareness, understanding, and knowledge about God, ourselves, and life in general—a state of thinking, feeling, and being. Whether we are awake or asleep, the engine of mind just keeps running, the power is eternally expressing, which means that every prayer of consciousness is answered. How can this be?

Looking particularly at the lower vibration of consciousness, we see that the prayer of the person living in poverty is impoverishment, the prayer of the sick person is illness, the prayer of those who are unsuccessful is failure. Why? Because that's where consciousness is. Same thing in the higher frequency: "For to him who has will more be given; and from him who has not, even what he has will be taken away" (Matthew 25:29). Regardless of the vibration, the tone of consciousness is always played in the phenomenal world.

The examples are endless. An addict craves addiction. A victim "prays" to be the target of others. Loneliness produces loneliness. Boredom breeds boredom. One who lives with frustration is calling for futility. Oversensitiveness brings irritation. Fear magnetizes that which is feared. Like attracts like. We are what we think about all day long, said Emerson.

"But I am not totally immersed in negativity," you may say. "There are good days and some that are not so good in body, mind, and pocketbook." Yes, consciousness can move in and out of the clouds, bright one day, cloudy the next—just like the weather. We always demonstrate what our inner convictions are at any given time.

"But I pray to God to take care of my problems," you may argue. The power of God can only do for us what it can do through us. To change anything "out there," we must first change what's inside—in consciousness.

Because of human nature, that would be almost impossible—like pulling ourselves up by our own bootstraps. Fortunately, there is a Presence and Power within us that can help us change our consciousness, and thus every aspect of our lives. I am referring, of course, to the Spirit of God individualized in us, as the reality of our being, and the causal powers that constitute our divine identity.

To correct your consciousness, turn it toward the Light within, becoming aware that God-As-Self is right where you are. You can remind yourself, "Knowing that everything I experience in the outer world is in strict accordance with my state of mind and emotions, it is my intention to change my consciousness—to think and feel rightly, and to see only that which I want expressed in my life and affairs. But I know that I cannot do this alone. I need your help."

With this acknowledgment you relax into the everlasting Energy of infinite Lovingness and feel the warmth and tenderness of that sacred Presence as you wait in the silence. You don't think about problems; you think only about the mighty Solution within. After a time you can get up and go about your business, and the angels will send impressions, intuitions, ideas, and instructions.

It is important to remember that the angels work in many different ways. Sometimes their "hands" seem to perform feats of incredible strength, and their ability to bring energy into form can amaze us. But the point I want to stress here is their genius for providing sudden flashes of thought—in a minimum of words—to jog us out of our lethargy and help us become clear and spiritually firm in consciousness.

Mary in Nevada makes this very clear. In a letter to me, she wrote:

Every morning during meditation, I make it a special point to greet the Holy Spirit within and my angels and to ask them to gather round. Then the messages begin, very often before I get out of bed, or maybe during the waking hours in the middle of the night. These are usually one-liners, very clear, to the point, and I make sure to remember them and put them to good use.

The messages could be about anything, but usually they will pertain to something I have been thinking-wondering-puzzling about. I know it's the angels communicating with me directly. I do not necessarily identify them specifically; I just thank them and put the messages to work. I'm eternally grateful and they know it.

I've also experienced this form of communication. For example, during one particular time in my life, I seemed to be trapped and found it almost impossible to relax and become centered. When I finally did turn within and asked for help in changing my consciousness, I heard the words "*Watch yourself.*" With this instruction came the understanding that I was being advised to step away from myself and look at the trend of my thoughts, to listen to my words, to monitor my emotions, and to watch my actions. I did, and was a bit shocked at what I was putting out.

Another admonishment came later that same day: "*Believe in yourself.*" I was being reminded again of my state of mind at the time, and how I felt as an individual in this world. You see, if we are filled with self-doubt and feelings of unworthiness, it is going to be difficult to lift our consciousness to a higher frequency. But I was also reminded of an affirmative prayer given to us in different versions of the Bible to correct our belief system: "I can do all things through Christ which strengtheneth me" (King James Version); "I can do all things in him who strengthens me" (Harper's Revised Standard Version); and "I am ready for anything through the strength of the one who lives within me" (the New Testament in Modern English, translated by J. B. Phillips). These words from Phil. 4:13—"I can do all things" and "I am ready for anything"—refer to the person who has found the Center within, the Truth, and who has embodied in consciousness this victorious Power.

Start believing in yourself and know beyond a shadow of a doubt that there is nothing that you cannot do, be, or have.

"*Stir up your faith*" was another instruction heard, and this ties into what you believe about yourself. Faith means confidence, trust, certainty, conviction. It is the Angel of Service and Synthesis in action, flooding your consciousness with "nothing is impossible" energy. Work with that angel to impress the truth on your mind and heart.

Another impression that came into my mind during that dark period was "*Regardless of your state of consciousness, that which was troubling you has already been taken care of. The situation has been healed. It has been since the moment you felt the emotion of the difficulty. Now lift your consciousness and prove to yourself that the problem no longer exists in the outer world.*"

I believe that it was the Angel of Illusion and Reality who provided this message, and the significance of it is that when we move in consciousness into the spiritual realm, we see that the challenge we thought we had is no longer there. At least that was the situation in my case—but I didn't know that at the time, and in my ignorance the difficulty was held in the mental–emotional system, projected out as a mirage, and judged as real.

Still later an angel said, "*Don't give up. Be persistent in reconditioning consciousness.*" I guess that I was becoming frustrated with my seeming inability to become a clear and open channel for spirit. If that's happened to you, remind yourself that you must be persistent in your spiritual work and follow a daily plan of consciousness conditioning. That can take the form of meditation, practicing the Presence, having meaningful dialogues with the angels, affirmative prayer, loving more, expressing gratitude, seeing a higher perspective through controlled visualization—do what works, and keep at it until you are clear and clean.

This idea of not giving up was emphasized again after Jan and I had visited our youngest daughter, Leslie, in France. Upon our return, we received a letter from her with this story:

The tiny restaurant where we had lunch in Villeneuve Loubet is named La Petite Votel. I asked my secretary what Votel meant, as it is not in the dictionary. She said that Votel was the famous chef of Louis XIV. He supervised all of the many cooks. While Louis ate a normal-sized meal, he would have hundreds of dishes cooked, then would choose from them for his dinner. Of course, all the platters would be paraded out for him to view. Votel oversaw all this and was famous for his beautiful and delicious dishes.

However, one day Votel went to the harbor to get some fresh fish for one of the dishes. There was a terrible storm, and the ship did not come in with the fish. Votel was so upset about this (and of course very fearful about not having the fish for dinner) that he killed himself.

But the really sad part is that shortly after he killed himself, the ship came in. It had only been delayed by the storm."

How many times have you given up just before your "ship" came in? It may have been delayed for a time because of the stormy sea of your emotions, but it was still on its way. And then you lost faith. This quitting released a surge of negative energy that reached out and turned the ship around and returned it to its point of origin. Your good had almost arrived, but you gave up.

Keep telling yourself, "The ship is coming, the ship is coming." Don't give up.

Another time when I was feeling a bit discouraged, I heard the words *"What do you really want in life?"* Now, that's a big one, and the question made me think about bringing things into tighter focus—not as unfulfilled desires, but as loving aspirations for this particular life.

Are you too embarrassed to tell yourself what you really want? Do you feel that you are degrading your spirituality if you include something "material," or an experience called "physical"? Sometimes we all forget that living in a material world demands energy-in-form and physical experiences. This doesn't mean that we are less spiritual. In fact, it will enhance our spirituality as we realize the unity of the invisible and the visible, of mind and manifestation.

Now back to the question: What do you really want in life? Open your journal and put your aspirations in writing. These will be your clear intentions, which, with warm feelings of love and joy, will be lifted to the level of great expectations—and then to fulfillment.

Someone whom I greatly respect once told me that there is no excuse for not being happy. I agree, for happiness and sorrow are only states of consciousness. And with the help of the angels, consciousness can be changed— if we are willing to change.

The energy of faith is truly a miracle-working power. Let's tap into it with this meditation.

The Will of God is flowing through me this very moment, dissolving all obstacles to joyous fulfillment.

The Love of God is helping me this day to stake my claim to the divine inheritance of All Good.

The Wisdom of God is filling my consciousness and guiding me in every activity of my life.

The Inspiration of God is quickening me to do that which is mine to do—and I gladly do it.

I give myself over, completely, to the Will, Love, Wisdom, and Inspiration of God.

I have the faith to move mountains because I AM the Power of Faith. I believe! I have total confidence, trust, certainty, and conviction in the Divine Process working in and through me now.

FIVE

Communication with
Angels in Dreams

In the book *Dream Symbolism* by Manly P. Hall, we read:

> A vast amount of knowledge that we now consciously hold
> came to us first as the result of sleep phenomena. The ancients
> held that most knowledge came from the gods; that man was
> first instructed by divine beings; and this is little more than
> saying that this knowledge came to man not merely from his
> own experience, but by revelation. The dream is therefore a
> valid form of revelation, and has always been so regarded.[1]

Knowledge and revelations from the gods, or angels, during times of slumber have been the experience of many people for eons, for the agents of Spirit within us do not sleep. They are continually active, particularly when the conscious mind withdraws from the stress and strain of the day and enters into the sleep state. This retiring from the evidence of the senses provides the angels with the opportunity to answer questions for us, to offer guidance, and to quicken our spiritual development through impressions of divine principles. As Joseph Campbell put it, "All the gods are within us. This is the great realization of the Upanishads of India in the ninth century B.C. All the gods, all the heavens, all the worlds, are within us." He added, "The dream is an inexhaustible source of spiritual information about yourself. . . . You can interpret a personal dream by association, figuring out what it is talking about in your own life, or in relation to your own personal problem."[2]

One of my former clients often sought guidance through his dreams to personal problems, declaring that his subconscious mind often revealed to him the answers. He said, "My batting average is fairly good, and many times I will awaken with a clear course of action that came to me in a dream." While this man was not familiar with the causal powers living just beyond his objective level of consciousness, he did have faith in what he called "the reservoir of great knowledge" within his subjective nature. Imagine what could have been revealed to him in dreams had he known about the twenty-two angels and had worked to free their "imprisoned splendor."

A man I met at a workshop in Minnesota had been working with the archetypes from *The Angels Within Us*, particularly the Angel of Discernment, and gave me this report.

I've kept a dream book beside my bed for years, writing down as fully as possible my dreams as soon as I woke up. Most were just symbolic representations of my own inner turmoil, the stuff that I was processing through. Then I started working with the angels, and soon Adonis (the Angel of Discernment) began coming into my dreams, identifying himself as the master of discrimination and offering advice regarding the operations of my company. Symbols and analogies were still used, but I seemed to be able to better interpret the messages. I attribute this to the angel energy.

Over a period of several weeks now I've had several nightly visits. One time I got the message that my plan for expansion was premature. Another time he implied that my marketing director was preparing to take another job paying more money. The angel also suggested that I tighten my operations, eliminate certain unprofitable lines, and keep my lead group by compensating them more. At least, that's my understanding. My wife thought I was crazy, but I followed the angel's advice and morale at the company has never been better. So are our profits.

Recall from the previous chapter my comment about the angels representing our own innate spiritual powers—qualities of divine force that make up our consciousness, our very selfhood. Also remember that these Living Energies are subject to our ego projections, which means that they may have to resort to symbols and parables for dream communications. But, as suggested by the man in Minnesota, the angels will also assist in the interpretation of the dream after we awaken.

In writing about dream seminars at the Edgar Cayce Association for Research and Enlightenment, W. Lindsay Jacob, M.D., says, "A dream is a message from yourself to yourself. It is presented in disguised form *not* for the purpose of obscuring the information but for the purpose of getting the information past the smoke screen of one's beliefs, prejudices, misconceptions, and false self-image."[3]

A good example of this was given to me by Debra in Seattle, who had been in daily contact with the Angel of Loving Relationships to "arrange" the perfect life partner for her. She soon met a man at a party and felt that he was Mr. Right. However, the night after the second date she had a dream.

I was running down this high hill to what looked like a valley below, where Charles was standing with arms wide open. It seemed like a beautiful spring day on the hill—lots of flowers and leafed trees—but when I reached level ground, I noticed that it was all desert, and the sand burned my feet. I continued running toward Charles when suddenly my angel appeared before me, blocking my way. Then I woke up.

Later I decided that Charles really wasn't the one for me when I learned from another woman that he can be very abusive, both emotionally and physically. I was heading down, down, into a burning, barren relationship, and thank heavens my angel saw this. I stopped seeing Charles, and a month later I started going with someone else. The Angel of Loving Relationships is smiling now, both in and out of my dreams.

And then there are those dreams in which lessons are taught and healings take place without the need for disguise, as shown in this letter from a woman in California.

I give a workshop to a group in Santa Barbara on a monthly basis. They called themselves The Angel Group long before I became involved. Christmas came around and I told them all about your book, The Angels Within Us. *They were thrilled and asked if I would give workshops on each angel. I agreed because it would allow me to work with the angels, which I had not yet done.*

As I was putting together a plan for the first workshop, I realized that I must be the facilitator for the healing/cleansing meditation, as well as for the meditation to meet the Angel of Unconditional Love and Freedom. Feeling the need to fill my own spiritual vessel, I wished that I could be the student on the morrow rather than the leader. And present also was no small guilt that I had not done the work before I was to assist others.

Oh, me of little faith! I went to bed and experienced the most lucid dream, brighter and more alive than the usual dream state. In very clear vignettes I saw my fear of growing old and losing my identity, my guilt for not taking better care of my physical body, my fear of the world not always being the same.

It was very clearly shown to me that it was time to let go of the past— what we know as history, tradition, roots, and lineage. It is no longer pertinent. History will be no longer. If held too tight, lineage and tradition can separate us from each other. Identity comes from a larger understanding.

More transforming than that was when I looked into a mirror and an old, gray-haired woman looked back at me. I looked into my own eyes and did not know myself. Then an immense cleansing, forgiving, and healing process took place. I was gently and lovingly guided by Spirit and the Angel of Unconditional Love and Freedom to clarity, understanding, and release.

Rather than being exhausted by the work I had done in the dream, I was energized and felt light and free. I am ever grateful for freedom from the past and all its baggage—and freedom from fear of the future, not to mention a myriad of other issues. And the next day's workshop? It was POWERFUL! Without question I was in a much better place, having already had my own work done. And without question, it is easier to call forth the energies when you have personal knowledge of them.

Thank you, Angel of Unconditional Love and Freedom, for your love and guidance on so many levels. You knew my need and filled it, allowing me to better assist others. And how clever of you to use the dream state.

Another form of dream is one in which clues are given as if to solve a mystery. Dr. Jacob calls this "an intriguing kind of riddle that titillates the imagination, which in turn almost automatically draws us to attempt to solve it."[4] I have had two such experiences that would fall into this category, each involving a series of vivid dreams about our dog.

What does a dog story have to do with working with the angels? The angels understand our needs, heart's desires, and what will make us feel whole in certain aspects of our lives. Jan and I experienced a great loss when our dog died, and knowing that loss attracts even more loss, the angels went to work to bring things into order and harmony again. They created a night-time mystery complete with clues, and as we followed each one as revealed in the dreams, we soon had our dog back with us. And the guidance was perfect down to the last detail.

Keep in mind that the angels can appear in any disguise to bring us messages; they will do whatever is necessary to capture our attention. And while the voice wasn't important in the dreams cited below, the angels can certainly duplicate the speech of a loved one for maximum impact and remembrance. In our case, the angel simply acted as a role-playing messenger working telepathically between one soul energy and another.

In *The Angels Within Us*, I briefly mentioned the "Brandy-Maggi" story—the amazing dream episodes involving our beloved springer spaniel—and the adventure on both sides of the veil has continued into 1994. It was the Angel of Order and Harmony who was responsible for relaying the meaningful information during this incredible journey, and I will be forever grateful to this angel for proving to me and Jan that life is eternal—and that dogs do indeed have souls.

To give you the full benefit of the first story, originally told in my book *Practical Spirituality*,[5] I'll go back to the evening of July 17, 1981. Jan and I had been watching an uplifting movie on television, when suddenly my heart became so heavy that I had to get up and go outside. I sat down beside our dog, Brandy, who was as much a part of our lives as our own children, and for over an hour I cried like a baby. I had no idea why I was so grief-stricken, and it wasn't until the next morning that I knew.

While we were having breakfast, Brandy was on the floor between us, and we both noticed that she was having difficulty breathing. We picked her up and drove to the vet as quickly as possible, but within minutes after our arrival, she died. Then I knew what I had been "told" the night before, and the grief came back like a tidal wave, engulfing both of us. The tears flowed for the rest of the day and into the night, and the next morning there was still no relief.

Two nights later I had a dream. I could see Brandy through a thin curtain. I was on one side and she was on the other, and she was trying desperately to claw her way through. I woke up, shook Jan, and told her that we must release Brandy at once, that our grief was holding her from her highest good. We did, and with very wet eyes, went back to sleep.

A few days later an unusual sequence of dreams began, each about a week apart. In the first one I was walking down a country road and Brandy came running up beside me, saying, "Tell Mommy I'm coming back." And I said (for some strange reason), "That's not her name; her name is Jan." Brandy replied, "But you always called her Mommy in front of me." Then she ran off down the road. I didn't say anything to Jan the next morning. After all, it was only a dream.

In the second dream, I was walking down that same country road and here came Brandy again, almost hollering this time: "You didn't tell Mommy that I'm coming back!" I just smiled at her, and she said, "You'd better tell her, because I'm coming back on October 20."

Well, you can imagine what happened when the alarm went off the next morning. I said, "Jan, I've got something to tell you, something a bit strange, but I've been told that I'd *better* tell you." I then reviewed both dreams. Jan just looked at me and didn't say anything.

About a week later I had the third dream. This time I was leaning against a fence talking to Brandy, and another springer spaniel ran up. I leaned down to pat her, and Brandy said, "Be careful, she's four years old." I asked, "What does that mean?" And she replied, with a big grin on her face, "You'll know."

In the next dream Brandy and I were walking down that country road again, talking like two old friends. (She was walking upright and was as tall as I was.) She said, "By the way, I'm changing my consciousness this time." I stopped, looked right into her eyes, and asked, "But why? I love you the way you are." She responded, "Oh, I'll still be the same dog, the same soul, but I don't want to have another heart attack, so I am changing my consciousness."

In dream number five Brandy told me to "look for the white," and in the final dream, a week later, she was very emphatic in saying, "Don't try to find me. Don't do anything. It's all been worked out, so don't run around looking for me. You'll know!"

In September, our oldest daughter, Susan, moved in with us briefly, bringing her huge cat, Puff, with her. When she arrived, Jan noticed a deep scratch on the cat and suggested that Puff be taken to the vet. While she and Susan were there, the vet asked, "Jan, are you and John ready for another dog yet?" Jan, being very cautious, said, "I don't know . . . we'll just wait and see." The vet said, "Well, if you decide you want another springer, here's the name and telephone number of a woman whose dog is going to have a litter."

Jan took the information and that night called the woman. Jan asked, "When are the pups due?" The woman answered, "October 20." We got goose bumps. The woman added, "This is my springer's first litter." Jan asked, "How old is your dog?" The reply: "Four years old."

We were right on target at this point but couldn't do anything else until the pups were born. When we heard that the baby springers had arrived, Jan and I went right over and were soon kneeling over a box filled with wet-nosed pups. In the middle of the litter was a female with huge white patches over a background of liver brown. We immediately put in our claim for *that* one (Brandy had said "Look for the white"), and visited her constantly until we could bring her home.

Brandy always had an unusual way of greeting us. She would sit down on her haunches and raise her two front paws in the air—in almost a "take me I'm yours" kind of posture. When the new pups were four weeks old, we went to visit them one Sunday afternoon. They were all out playing on the lawn. As we got out of our car and walked across the grass, the little white-and-brown one turned, saw us coming, managed to get up on her rear end, and held her paws up high—just like Brandy used to do. This almost did Jan in, and she ran across the yard squealing, "My baby, my baby!"

We named the pup Magnificent Brandy Too, and called her Maggi for short. She stayed with us for over twelve years.

Now for the second dream sequence. In November 1993, Maggi became ill, and her condition worsened over a period of about two weeks. We worked with her on all levels—medicine from the vet, prayers, spiritual healing, and finally releasing her to Spirit. Then, during the early morning hours of December 4, I had a dream. I saw a big dog biscuit suspended in midair, up close to the ceiling of our living room. I noticed that Maggi saw it too. She leaped for it, soaring over the couch and catching it in her mouth, then continued right up and disappeared through the top of the house. When I woke up with the dream fresh in my mind, I knew she was gone.

I quietly got out of bed and went into the living room. Maggi was stretched out in her favorite sleeping position. The body was there, but she wasn't. I put my hand on her beautiful head and wished her a glorious trip into the Light, then went back and woke up Jan.

We didn't go back to sleep that night—too much to do, to talk about, to remember. But that's not the end of the story.

On December 30, 1993, Jan also took a journey into the Light. She had been experiencing pain in her arms and chest that morning, and since we don't have a doctor, I called EMS. Within minutes after they arrived, the EKG monitor went flat-line, and I heard one of the paramedics yell, "We've lost her!" Jan had suffered a massive heart attack and died on the stretcher. She was gone for several minutes until brought back with electric paddles. She remembers leaving her body, watching all the commotion below, then being lifted up by angelic beings and taken to the other side for a most remarkable healing and learning experience.

Guess who was there to meet her. Always standing by on the other side of the veil to greet the newcomer is the deepest love connection, and to Jan, that was Maggi. She and Maggi spent much time together "over there" as two souls in loving communication. Jan soon recuperated and was able to return home. On the first day home from the hospital, as she was sitting in her meditation chair, Jan physically felt a big wet kiss and knew it was Maggi. Shortly after this incident, I started having the dreams.

In one, Maggi was wearing a coat of diamonds, but she didn't say anything. In another dream she said to me, "I'll be coming back soon, and you can't make a mistake in finding me. It will be so easy, so easy." Then in early April I dreamed that I was reading the Austin newspaper (we regularly get the San Antonio paper), and suddenly Maggi emerged from out of the paper. I woke up and told Jan that we had to find an Austin paper, that Maggi was going to be born in Austin again. We checked the paper every day, and not a springer spaniel anywhere.

In mid-April I dreamed that I was looking at the want ads in the Austin paper, and there in bold print were these words: "Championship sire." We checked the paper that day. Nothing.

Over a month passed and not another dream. Then, on the night of May 21, a black-and-white springer spaniel walked through my dream without speaking. I knew it wasn't Maggi, but my first thought upon awakening was "something's happening."

The next morning, Sunday, we drove to the store to buy an Austin paper. As I was putting the quarters into the paper dispenser, my hands started shaking. I jerked the newspaper out and quickly turned to the want ads. There in bold print was "Springer Spaniel puppies. Beautifully marked. *Champion sired.*" Those last two words tied in almost perfectly with the dream.

We drove home and called the number in the ad. The puppies were four and a half weeks old, born on April 28. The woman who answered said that the father was black and white (that's who I saw in the dream), the mother liver and white, with all the pups having the mother's coloring. We made arrangements to see them that afternoon, and the address in Austin was Easy Street. (Remember that Maggi had emphasized to me how "easy" it would be to find her.)

An hour and a half later we were kneeling beside the whelping box and looking at six beautiful springer puppies. We picked up each one, finally getting to a female. As Jan picked her up, the pup began licking Jan's face profusely (none of the others had done that) while making a cooing sound. Jan had a huge smile on her face as she handed the dog to me, and I went through a similar kissing experience.

The owner then said, "We call her Diamond because of the diamond marking on her back." I instantly remembered the dream about the coat of diamonds. When I looked into the pup's eyes, I knew for sure that it was Maggi. Same eyes, much more mature looking than the other pups, and she wouldn't stop staring at me—seeming to say, "Don't mess up now . . . it's really me."

We told the woman that we'd take the diamond pup, and Jan was about to make out a check when a male pup came up and started making grunting sounds at her. We picked him up, and Jan said, "Maybe we ought to get two. That way Maggi would have company when we travel." It sounded good to me.

Maggi's official name is Lady Maggi Diamond. The male pup is Sir Casey McAlister, Casey for short. It's so good to have her back, and bringing a friend with her is a double treasure.

Did an angel act out the role of Brandy/Maggi in the dreams? I believe that the archetypal energy in me that corresponded to our dog was the Angel of Order and Harmony, because that's what Brandy brought to us when she came into our lives in the early 1970s. And that same energy was projected as the dog on the screen of my consciousness in the dreams.

Thank you, Athena, for speaking to us as the beautiful soul of our dog, for knowing every detail of the rebirth scenarios, and for playing your part so well.

I relax and let the cares of the busy day be lifted from me.
All tension is flowing out, all stress relieved, and I am
entering the calm sea of tranquility. It is the moment to be
still, a time for rest, for solitude and serenity, to be at peace
with myself and with my world.

At ease physically, mentally, and emotionally, I am
ready for that blessed sweet slumber where angels minister
to me without interference. I lovingly invite these agents of

Spirit to guide and direct me in vivid, meaningful dreams, to reveal to me my highest purpose, and to show me the way of joyful fulfillment in life.

When I awaken, I will remember their visit, the words of wisdom given to me, the practical advice offered, and the unfailing promise of their voice and hands ever guiding and guarding me on my journey of life.

I close my eyes now and gently fall into the deep hush of restful sleep.

SIX

The Angel Fire
of Purification

How many of us have started out on the spiritual path with the primary objective of solving personal problems? Probably everyone reading this book. We began our metaphysical studies seeking answers to the questions of life and hoping to fulfill our desires, yet often the healings of body, pocketbook, and relationships soon followed.

After a time, however, the extraordinary demonstrations of a new state of consciousness came to a halt. It seemed that we had found the keys to the kingdom, but when we weren't looking, someone had changed the locks. What really happened? The initial cause of our problems—the patterns in our emotional nature—continued to be active, stimulating periodic cycles of return and bringing old trials and tribulations to the surface to be faced once again.

Until we transform our lower nature—specifically, the error patterns on the unconscious level and our known personality defects—it will be difficult for us to completely awaken to a life of harmony and remain in that higher energy. As I have written elsewhere, the first principle in the awakening process is renunciation: "It is such a critical course of action that not a single mystery school, religion, esoteric teaching, or spiritual philosophy omitted it from [its] traditional disciplines."[1] Renunciation is followed by a mystical death and rebirth, a transmutation of the personality to loosen the grip of ego so that we may begin the ascension to superconsciousness.

Who are responsible for helping us give up our mortal sense of existence so that we may become identified with all that is good, true, and beautiful in life? None other than the Angel of Renunciation and Regeneration and the Angel of Death and Rebirth. The energy of renunciation is the Neptune archetype, which is associated with water, the washing away of malevolent thought forms. The energy of metamorphosis—the death and rebirth archetype—continues the process with what seems to be a fiery experience. As the old error states of consciousness are dissolved by the mighty flow of purifying energy, the baptism by fire follows to burn away the parent thoughts and emotions that created the negative patterns in the first place.

In *Fragments of a Faith Forgotten*, we read that "when a man receiveth the mysteries of the baptisms, those mysteries become a mighty fire, exceedingly fierce, wise, which burneth up sins; they enter into the soul secretly and devour all the sins which the counterfeit spirit hath implanted in it."[2]

When we reach the point at which we truly desire to exchange the lesser for the greater, the angel will begin to work through all levels of consciousness to prepare us for the spiritual rebirth, as indicated in this letter that I received.

During the past few weeks my consciousness, mind, and physical body have been subjected to numerous surges of fire, of brilliant, blazing, white-hot fire. These fiery purifications have burned away nearly all traces of lower energy and darkness from the cells of my physical body, and have also removed old fears. I know now that people make a terrible error when they deny their own divinity, when they believe that they cannot perform the greatest of miracles for the benefit of all living things. If necessary, one person alone could transform the entire planet Earth, simply because each of us is blessed with Divine Power, Divine Wisdom, and above all, Divine Love.

And here is an experience directly related to the work of the angels, as reported by Gene of Kansas City:

I have used every metaphysical formula written, and I continued to suffer from just about any problem you could name. When I read your Angel *book, I started with the Angel of Abundance. It took some time to make meaningful contact, but when I did I received a very direct instruction. She said, "I can't do a thing for you until you clean up your act." When I asked what I should do, she said, "Forgive your mother . . . seek purification of the past."*

She didn't mention the Angel of Renunciation and Regeneration or the Angel of Death and Rebirth by name, and it wasn't until I got to those chapters that I realized there were energies that could help me. When I called for purification by the angels, Renunciation appeared to me, standing in a waterfall, and asked me to come into his presence. I was afraid, but I went to him and embraced him, and I immediately felt something happening within me. After a few minutes I fell asleep, and when I woke up the bedsheets were soaking wet. I felt weak and completely drained.

Since then some things have changed. For one thing, a week after my experience I received a raise in pay, and for another, my mother called. We hadn't spoken in over a year. But there are still other areas that are causing distress. Where do I go from here?

The angels of purification can work best for us when we take the necessary steps to lift our consciousness, so the only place to go is up. Keep in mind that the angels aren't a group of "fixers" who come in and solve our every problem without any work on our part. Their role is to free us as we free them, so it's up to us to make the first move. And when we are finally attuned to their higher vibration through our dedication to living the spiritual life, we will find that they do indeed straighten crooked places in consciousness, perfect that which concerns us, and perform that which is ours to do. But first things first.

In thinking about "the only place to go is up," I am reminded of the biblical story of the prodigal son. If you recall, it is not the father in that story who goes to look for the son; the son initiates the action. Luke 15:11–32 tells about a wealthy young man who gathers his inheritance and runs off to a far country to lead a loose life. He eventually gets into trouble, goes broke, experiences starvation, and winds up working as a hired hand feeding pigs.

Finally, the young man comes to himself and says, "I will arise and go to my father." Notice that he doesn't beg God to be delivered from his plight. And when no one will give him anything, he doesn't try to manipulate others. Oh, he could tell the farmer that he winds up working for that he is the son of a rich man, and that he will have him well compensated later for a little charity now. But he doesn't do that.

He could tell himself, "I'll use the power of my mind to change all of this"—and let's say he affirms, visualizes, and speaks the word for something miraculous to happen. Perhaps in a few hours the owner of the farm comes out to the field and says, "Here are a few table scraps to fill your belly, and since you seem to be a decent chap, you can sleep in the barn. Keep up the good work and I'll put you on minimum wage."

This will have delighted the young man. Can't you just hear him saying, "Boy, do I have the power! This mind stuff works—talk about a miracle!" But from our vantage point we can see that in this scenario, the prodigal son would only be playing the game of substitution, exchanging an unfavorable appearance for one a little more to his liking—changing one illusion for another.

He also could look at his situation in this way: "I'll get up and go home and ask my father to come back to the pigpen with me—to clean it up and make it beautiful, harmonious, and fit for pleasurable living." Haven't we all done that? We try to use God-power to change an effect in the physical world, rather than eliminate the barriers in our mental-emotional nature.

The point of this story is none of the above. The line that says "he comes to himself" means that he suddenly realizes that he doesn't have to live this way, that he has a choice. He also knows that wherever he goes on the physical plane, he takes his consciousness with him, so he doesn't try to run away to another town or country to start over. That would mean a repeat of the same old conditions at some point in time. He knows that the only real journey is within—spiritually up—and this upward movement is told in the before and after: "I will arise. . . . And he arose." The very instant we commence the inner journey, we are beginning our transformation from humanhood to Divine Selfhood.

The moment of surrender is told in Luke 15:18–19: "I will arise and go to my father, and I will say to him, 'Father, I have sinned against heaven and before you; I am no longer worthy to be called your son; treat me as one of your hired servants.' "

This "giving up" opens the door to the Angel of Renunciation and Regeneration, who helps to maintain consciousness in the surrender mode for the initial cleansing. This may seem to take place almost instantaneously—as evidenced by the prodigal's experience and in this letter:

I was in a situation that I could not find peace and I finally, and fitfully, surrendered. I just gave up. In that simple act of heartfelt surrender I "snapped" and my world changed. After that experience I knew that when I died, I would die happy because I had the knowledge that God was real.

When we have no place else to go, we surrender to the higher power within. That's the starting point for purification, the trigger mechanism for the angels. When the prodigal son realizes he can't do it alone, he is consenting to receive the purifying energy, which initiates his rise in consciousness. His loving, all-knowing Master Self then rushes toward the ascending energy and encompasses it. In the story the son's rehearsed speech about unworthiness is later ignored by the father, who directs his servants to immediately prepare a great feast to celebrate his son's return.

Perhaps the moral of the story of the prodigal son is that "God helps those who help themselves." We take the first step, and the angels take it from there to lead us into higher consciousness. Sometimes they give us very graphic illustrations of what we must do, as shown in this letter:

In meditation I asked what I could do to help me move up higher. After a few minutes in the silence, a voice said, "I am expressing the fullness of my Christhood." I was immediately filled with questions like who and how. Shortly I saw many pairs of hands coming out of the darkness, each pair moving rhythmically up and down like scales seeking equilibrium. And the voice said, "Maintain perfect balance."

Implicit in the words was the greater understanding of not just balancing the physical and spiritual, but of giving up judgment, of being totally allowing. As the pairs of hands faded I found myself watching a long line of men and women chained together. Each was chained by one ankle to the person in front and chained by the other ankle to the person in back. Each person's right hand was on the right shoulder of the person in front. Cov-

ered in sweat and dirt with their heads bowed down, they trudged in lock-step up the hills. The line went down and up and down as far back into the sunset as I could see—into infinity.

The voice then said, "Separate yourself from others." I spent a great deal of time pondering and meditating on all three messages. Finally I realized that I had been putting off my life until I was more evolved or good enough. I understood what the messages were about—making a commitment to Christhood. I have.

I have found that the first step in breaking the chains of gravity and ensuring the cooperation of the angels of purification is to do what we can to balance the physical, emotional, and mental bodies. Let's take the physical body first.

If we are primarily physically oriented, we tend to be a bit fanatical, not only about our own bodies but about what other people are doing with theirs. Physically focused people of this world are usually zealots about food, diet, certain forms of exercise, every kind of nutritional supplement, and a variety of regimens relating to health. This overemphasis on the physical form calls for constant monitoring of the system and frequently leads to feelings of discomfort because of overstimulation of the energy centers. Consciousness then focuses its attention on where the problem seems to be, which in turn channels concerned energy to the affected area, increasing the potency of the problem.

Before considering the emotional body, let's make a distinction between emotions and feelings. Emotions are reactive, a negative state of consciousness concentrated in the solar plexus. Feelings, on the other hand, are the warmth of Spirit being expressed as love, joy, peace, and so on, from the heart center. The highly reactive people of this world live primarily in the emotional body below the heart and are subject to periods of morbid introspection, fear, anger, guilt, unmanageable desires, and self-pity.

Riding on top of the emotional system in the auric field is the mental body. If too much energy is concentrated there, we overanalyze, overorganize, and overengineer everything, and have a tendency to argue with anyone who has a different point of view. Mentally focused individuals place much emphasis on their particular definition of tradition, sometimes becoming a bit radical in defense of their mind-sets.

Most of us are not exclusively physical, emotional, or mental, but instead have periods during which we emphasize one aspect in our general personality makeup. The idea, again, is *balance.* We should enjoy the physical body for what it is—a vehicle for consciousness on the material plane—and care for it lovingly without fanaticism.

We also should make it a daily practice to focus more on feelings of love and joy. The news of the day cannot be ignored, but world events should be seen without registering anger or fear.

Finally, we should be aware that when we take depression and self-absorbed brooding into a contemplative state, we are causing a deep disturbance in the emotional system, which will be expressed outwardly in some way. The following letter from a schoolteacher in Michigan makes this clear. Fortunately, one of the angels in this circumstance was sufficiently free to intervene and bring this individual out of the darkness.

One night the guilt from an operation that I had had when I was thirty, and the emotional residue from my mother's death when I was twenty-two, came up in a terrible sense of grief. I felt way over my limit—and my head—and my life seemed very bleak and desolate. I decided I wanted to end it. My husband had several different guns in the house, and I began to consider which one to use. I felt so alone and helpless with no one to comfort me. Then, as I was choosing my weapon, an overwhelming energy filled the room. It literally made the hair on my head and arms stand on end. At that moment the most beautiful angel walked in. He was swirling wheels of energy in blues, greens, silvers, and golds. He vibrated constantly with swirling energy. Instantly I felt great overpowering love. He was the Angel of Unconditional Love to free me of my emotions. I felt peaceful and very loved. All thoughts of suicide were gone, and I was healed. I went back to bed, slept, and felt marvelous the next day.

Here you can see that the angels work together. In this case, with surrender out of the question due to out-of-control emotions, the Angel of Renunciation and Regeneration was blocked, as was the Angel of Death and Rebirth, who could have helped this woman see "true death" in the sense of a change in consciousness. So the unconditional love archetype took over to free her from the gripping emotions—and literally save her life.

———

In working with our mental system, we should realize that an overtaxing of the faculties of the mind is counterproductive. We should shift into neutral more and let the answers, solutions, and ideas flow easily from the deeper realm of consciousness. We also should practice harmlessness, discuss things constructively with others without criticism, and not be so exclusive in our thinking.

As we come more into balance physically, emotionally, and mentally, we are ready for the second step in purifying our consciousness for the lift up—and that is to surrender to the Master Self.

Relax, become centered, and say the following:

> *At this moment in time, I willingly consent to the Holy*
> *Presence within and totally surrender without reservation to*
> *Its Power, Love, and Intelligence.*

This submission not only brings us into alignment with the water and fire of the angel baptism, but also leads us into the rhythm of Wholeness where everything works in harmony for our highest good.

Ralph Waldo Emerson wrote, "There is a principle which is the basis of things, which all speech aims to say, and all action to evolve, a simple, quiet, undescribed, undescribable presence, dwelling very peacefully in us, our rightful lord; we are not to do, but to let do; not to work, but to be worked upon; and to this homage there is a consent of all thoughtful and just people in all ages and conditions. To this sentiment belong vast and sudden enlargements of power. . . ."[3]

Say to yourself:

*I recognize the principle of all things, a quiet presence
dwelling very peacefully within me, my rightful lord. I am
not to do, but to let do; not to work, but to be worked
upon. I consent to this with all my heart and mind. Beloved
One, I am willing to give myself to You. I am willing to
have You live me. I seek nothing but You.*

We are here on earth as incarnated beings to be conscious channels for the Essential Self, our Divine Soul. This is not running away from life. It is entering life from the highest aspect and partaking of the supernal energies that are constantly lifting us above the emptiness and futility of the old humanhood, lifting our consciousness into higher and higher vibrations that we may experience the greater and grander realities of life.

As we are cleansed in consciousness, we move into the universal rhythm and begin to unfold. To unfold means to open up, unfurl, spread out, as a bud becoming the full flower.

Say to yourself:

*I am being lifted above the consciousness and experiences of
the past, and I am entering the highest aspect of life. I
consent to this. I am willing to unfold, to open naturally, in
the rhythm of the universal flow.*

*I let go. I release. I completely surrender to the Master
Mind of infinite Power, Love, and Intelligence within, and I*

accept that Mind as the Source and Cause of every activity
of my life. I consent to be used by this Holy Presence for Its
eternal fulfillment.

It takes humility to be used by Spirit—not modesty but humbleness, not self-abasement but reverence for the higher consciousness. And the "use" that we give It is our joyful willingness to be Its instrument without resistance. With this readiness, the Master within uses us to express and reveal wholeness in every aspect of our lives.

Say to yourself:

I am on the path of my own natural unfolding, and nothing
will deter me from this divine intention. If any miscreation
from the past surfaces to be dealt with, it will be handled
easily by the angels within, and I will rejoice in what seems
to be a miraculous happening in my life.

I give thanks and move forward in my unfolding
without tension and stress, for I know now that there is
nothing to worry about. I simply stay in the flow, rising
higher and higher in the radiant light, seeing everything
whole and perfect.

As we relax and surrender ourselves to be used by the Wholeness of Self, we are automatically released from the chains, pulls, and hooks of self-created effects and error patterns of the past. The Angel of Renunciation and Regeneration and the Angel of Death and Rebirth have gone to work, and we no longer have to tug at the chains that bind us; they just fall away and we find that we are free.

And we shall bloom as beautiful flowers, which are, as Longfellow said, "emblems of our own great resurrection."

SEVEN

The Angels Reveal the Truth

When we realize the Truth about ourselves, we are no longer just a "human being." We are lifted into the Light of Knowing, where our creative powers are essentially limitless, and life becomes a joyful and loving adventure of service and fulfillment.

Many of the angels assist in the realization process by providing the necessary energies to unite the lower and higher natures. Once the fusion takes place with the angels' cooperation, the Master Self is in total control of the personality, and truly, all things are made new in our lives. The old religionists talked about this as living in heaven while still on earth.

Of course, realization of Truth is by degree, but we can certainly see evidence of the angels at work and know—"by their fruits"—when someone is nearing the experience of total Oneness with the Holy Self. The energy of these awakened individuals is different, and the light in their eyes can be mesmerizing. On one of our trips to California, for instance, Jan was introduced to a woman at a gathering. They stood looking at each other, not saying a word, and as their eye contact continued for several minutes, a hush fell over the crowded room. Finally, Jan and this woman nodded to one another and began conversing.

Later we discovered that this woman was quite unusual. When she was young, she was very shy and preferred reading to playing. She said, "The stories of the saints mystified me. I craved to know how they felt, and I shared with them an intense, burning love for God." As she grew up, her constant prayer was that God's will be done through her. In this state of consciousness she has been the channel to bring dead animals back to life, heal one son who was critically injured in an accident and another son of spinal meningitis, and bring life into dead plants.

This woman was able to prove that all things are possible. "Yet," she said, "the events are really not very important if we stop to think that, aside from our unity with the universe, anything else is insignificant. Obedience to God's voice, true love of our fellow human beings, compassion, forgiveness, realization of our unity with all beings and with all creation—that is what life is really all about."

Jan and I also met another woman whom a minister had called "one of the most Christed beings on the planet," and I know that we experienced a definite shift in consciousness just by being in her presence. We felt that she was looking right through us, as if bypassing the form and personality and beholding the Truth within. She also seemed to talk in parables, which made little sense to us at the time. Later, when the meaning of her stories suddenly flashed in our minds, we realized that she was answering every question we had, both spoken and unspoken, in a way that would provide even greater understanding than mere straight-line statements. She was giving us information in "timed-release capsules," so to speak, to get past any preconceived ideas or particular mind-sets.

During our second visit with this woman we witnessed, in the presence of medical doctors, several incredible healings of minds and bodies. We have since verified reports of her miraculous multiplication of provisions— just as Jesus did with the loaves and fishes. When asked the source of her incredible power, she said simply, "The Truth."

In one of my early visits with the Angel of Truth and Enlightenment, I asked him to give me a higher understanding of Truth. He said, "Your Truth is what you believe, yet beyond belief is Knowing, and this is the light of liberty." Later he reminded me that Truth cannot be taught; it can only be realized through an experience in consciousness. He suggested that I review the ancient texts to deepen my realization, to find proven principles to ponder, and ask myself, "What is Truth?" I followed his advice.

I discovered that in the sixth century B.C., Lao-tzu, founder of Taoism, said, "Those who know do not tell, and those who tell do not know." I realized that his comment reflected the philosophy of the ancient mystery schools, which taught that Truth must be protected from bigotry and intolerance. This indirect communication continued for the most part through the thousand years of the Dark Ages. When the light broke through in the sixteenth century, the Truth was slowly unveiled for public view. In the meantime, however, the mystery of Truth flourished only in the secret societies and sacred academies.

Truth was first given to sleeping humanity in symbols, then in music and song, later in myths and legends, again in poetry and parables. The reason was that, until the Middle Ages reached their climax, the human mind could not readily accept Divine Truth as a direct statement of fact. The Truth had to be disguised to penetrate the deeper mind, and even then it lost much in its descent into language.

To show how the teachings of Truth were passed down through the ages, I begin with Hercules, the ancient Greek Son of God, and travel through the centuries to learn from Krishna, the Supreme Personality of the Godhead in Hinduism; Hermes Trismegistus, the Egyptian God of Wisdom and Letters; to Jesus, the Christian Son of God.

The "Twelve Labors of Hercules," which dates to 3000 B.C., was one of the first symbolic dramas used to portray the path of return to Truth. The tale's hero, Hercules, representing the archetype of Power and Authority, performed the twelve labors, from the capture of the man-eating mares to the seizing of the red cattle of Geryon. When the tasks were completed, Hercules' teacher said, "The jewel of immortality is yours. By these twelve labors have you overcome the human, and put on the divine. Home you have come, no more to leave."[1]

Next came the worship of Krishna (c. 2000 B.C.), an incarnation of Vishnu who was believed to establish the planetary sense of love and to sow the seeds of emotional control and purification in the consciousness of sleeping humanity. In the Bhagavad Gita, Krishna, expressing the Energy of Unconditional Love and Freedom, reminds us of ancient truth when he says: "I am the Self . . . seated in the hearts of all creatures. I am the beginning, the middle and the end of all things. . . . Of all sciences I am the spiritual science of the Self, and among logicians I am the conclusive truth."[2]

Of significance is the teaching of Hermes Trismegistus, the legendary author of the *Hermetica*, a body of work exploring magical, astrological, and alchemical doctrines. Hermes was a contemporary of Moses (c. 1300 B.C.). He is viewed by some as representing the Angel of Illusion and Reality. Manly Hall writes that "the appellation 'Thrice Greatest' [Trismegistus] was given to Hermes because he was considered the greatest of all philosophers, the greatest of all priests, and the greatest of all kings."

Hall quotes from the Hermetic writings:

> Thus preached Hermes, "O people of the earth, men born
> and made of the elements, but with the spirit of the Divine
> Man within you, rise from your sleep of ignorance! Be sober

and thoughtful. Realize that your home is not in the earth but in the Light. Why have you delivered yourselves over into death, having power to partake of immortality? Repent, and *change your minds.* Depart from the dark light and forsake corruption forever. Prepare yourself to climb through the Seven Rings and to blend your soul with the eternal light."[3]

Finally, of importance in the presentation of the Truth are the teachings of Jesus, who spoke as the embodiment of Truth and Enlightenment, and the writings of Paul, who expressed the energy of Death and Rebirth. The New Testament, if read with discernment, can represent a guide to enable us to move out of the shadows and into the Light of Truth.

In John 8:32, Jesus says, "You will know the truth and the truth will make you free." And what is this ultimate, freeing Truth? The *I AM* that we are is the Truth! We are Divine Beings of Light; our Reality is the Spirit of God individualized as each one of us. Jesus taught: "You are the light of the world" (Matt. 5:14); "The kingdom of God is in the midst of you" (Luke 17:21); and "I said, ye are gods . . ." (John 10:34). Paul wrote: "We have received not the spirit of the world, but the Spirit which is from God . . ." (1 Cor. 2:12) and "Do you not know that you are God's temple and that God's Spirit dwells in you?" (1 Cor. 3:18).

It is the realization of the Truth of our Divine Identity that sets us free.

Subsequent visits with the Angel of Truth and Enlightenment brought me many new revelations, particularly on the realization process. During one session, the angel said, "Spend less time contemplating the meeting of challenges and the overcoming of problems and more time meditating on the sacred Light within. There are no problems. A burden is felt only because of the belief that there is a burden; a difficulty exists only because it is in mind. Focus mind and heart only on Truth, and let the false beliefs dissolve."

The part of this instruction about "no problems" was later proved correct. Jan and I were in Minnesota in the spring of 1993 conducting a workshop, and during one break a young woman began to tell me about all the problems she was facing at home with her husband and children. For some reason, I interrupted her and said, "Wait a minute . . . you don't have any problems."

She looked at me for a moment without speaking, then said, "Oh, I didn't know that. Thank you."

Shortly after returning home we received this letter from her:

When you told me that I didn't have any problems, I felt this shiver go up and down my spine, and I thought, well, maybe I really don't. Later that day I realized that any and all problems in my life were of my own making, and I decided right there in the workshop to unmake them. When I returned home that evening, I came home to a different husband and two different children. I knew it was because I was different.

Another instruction from the Angel of Truth and Enlightenment was, "As long as you continue to think about duality, you will experience it." This made me think about all the times we say something like, "While I may be outwardly broke, on the spiritual level I am abundantly prospered," or "In truth, I am whole and perfect, despite what my body says." That's looking at two sides of the coin when in fact there isn't any coin. There is only God and God in expression, which means that there is only abundance, only perfection, only harmony—not only spiritually, but on all levels of existence.

The angel also revealed that the root cause of all of our seeming difficulties is the belief that our existence is essentially physical, the belief that we are not perfect. He made me understand that if we think of ourselves as physical beings living in a purely material universe—and identify with the pleasure and pain of that universe—we are trapping ourselves in limitation, decay, deterioration, and death. Why? Because we associate ourselves with those appearances, and through this identification we establish a belief in materiality and imperfection.

The angel said, "All is energy. Know only energy, omnipresent and invisible. See only energy manifest as form, yet identify with the energy and not the form, and consciousness will have dominion."

As we contemplate this idea we begin to understand the dynamics of consciousness—unlimited, unbound, infinite, and inclusive—and we are lifted into a higher frequency where our vision and knowing become purer. We see everything as God-Energy expressing in perfect ways according to

Divine Principle. It dawns on us that what God created as perfect can never be rendered imperfect, that wholeness is eternal, abundance a never-ending process of manifestation, harmony an indisputable fact of life. And we wonder why in the name of God did we ever entertain beliefs to the contrary.

As we come back into our normal frame of reference—the so-called material world—we see more of reality shining through the mist. The spiritual Real has been in consciousness all the time in all its fullness, and knowing more of the Truth of our Being has stripped away a part of the veil. What happens then? We feel well physically, stronger and more vital. There's more love, joy, and peace in our heart. Everything is in balance. And somehow, some way, not planned by us, the energy of abundance reveals infinite Plenty in the form of an all-sufficiency of money.

We were created by God and remain forever as a thought in the Mind of God, projected into individualized energy fields, yet never leaving the presence of our Creator. Even after we took on physical form, which created a sense of separation, there continued to be only perfection in our complete oneness with God.

Jesus said, "You, therefore, must be perfect, as your heavenly Father is perfect" (Matt. 5:48). This "must be perfect" does not imply that it is a requirement; it means that it is a *certainty*.

Frequently, the Angel of Unconditional Love and Freedom plays an important role in helping us realize our innate perfection. Wallace in

Florida sent me some writings from his spiritual journal, along with this letter:

I believe that my break-through, as far as understanding that I was not a mortal being, came from working with the Angel of Unconditional Love and Freedom. I was shaving one morning when I caught a glimpse of someone else in the bathroom. I turned around, saw no one, but heard in my mind—"Love is the transformative power. Begin to love yourself AS YOU ARE, and show others that you care about them."

That was in June 1993. I immediately began working with the energy of love day and night, and within a couple of months, I was not the same person. My whole life changed, and I believe that the lives of those around me did too—all for the better.

It is said that love perfects everything, and that is certainly obvious from this woman's letter:

At the age of five I had the experience of becoming aware that LOVE, the kind taught and lived by the Master Jesus and many others, was the healing energy for our bodies, minds, souls, relations, the whole works. I recognized that my true nature, as well as all others, was love. As I grew in understanding, so did the magnetic energy field—drawing those to me who needed healing in some way. Through this awareness I have never met one I did not love, even though I may not have liked their habits or personality. Now the healing energy flows and heals through no effort of my own, other than to be what I AM, have always been, now and forever—LOVE. What the man Jesus did, we all can do. I know. I have. If I can, all can—by be-

coming aware of who they are and what they are, and by claiming their divine inheritance.

Emerson wrote that "what we commonly call man, the eating, drinking, planting, counting man, does not, as we know him, represent himself, but misrepresents himself. Him we do not respect, but the soul, whose organ he is, would he let it appear through his action, would make our knees bend. When it breathes through his intellect, it is genius; when it breathes through his will, it is virtue; when it flows through his affection, it is love . . . all spiritual being is in man."[4]

As the sunbeam is one with the sun, so we can never be separated from our Source. We are eternally and permanently fused with God, in God's Love and Life, and God cannot dismiss us out of Mind. We are seen by the Mind of God as the perfect creations we are, and God cannot change Its Mind about us.

Sometimes the Angel of Creative Wisdom is the one who jolts us out of our sleep. Bob, a friend of mine in Texas, shared this experience:

After affirming for days that I was a divine being and master of my destiny, I heard, "Oh, stop it!" Did that shake me? Yeah! When I asked who spoke the words, I got, "Your Wisdom." Since I had read your Angel *book, I asked, "Are you the Angel of Creative Wisdom?"*

She said, "Yes, and I'm trying to tell you that what you are doing is silly. Does a flower have to convince itself that it is one? You are what you are, offspring of the Infinite. Rather than assert that you are divine, accept it. Just simply accept it."

Now I'm working on acceptance.

"We are indeed his offspring," notes the Acts of the Apostles (17:28), descendants of the Most High, a race of gods, some sleeping, some awake, known as philosophers, poets, historians, teachers, and the authors of the books of the world's great religions.

The distinction between the sleeping and awakened ones is told beautifully in Manly P. Hall's book *The Phoenix*:

> The mysteries taught that there are two kinds of men: those who are awake and those who are asleep. So, according to the Mysteries, the ignorant lie sleeping—sleeping through all eternity, sleeping as worlds are made, sleeping as worlds perish again, sleeping as nations rise, sleeping as empires fall. Surrounded by infinite opportunity and part of a plan based on infinite growth, those who are not initiated into the mystery of Reality sleep in their narrow coffins of egotism, selfishness, and unawareness through all the eternities of time and being!
>
> Those who are awake live in a world of infinite light, infinite wisdom, infinite beauty, infinite opportunity, and infinite progress. To such all things are good; to such there is no death, and gradually they ascend that ladder of stars leading to the footstool of Divinity itself. To these awakened ones the universe is home and the myriads of

stars and heavenly bodies are kindred hosts of celestial
beings. All the world is a laboratory of experimentation;
every stick and stone preaches a sermon, every living thing
teaches a lesson.[5]

The angels are working at every moment to awaken us and help us discover the Great Self within. As we stir from our slumber, all twenty-two
causal powers begin to unite as one blazing light, radiating throughout our
auric field and shifting our consciousness into the fourth dimension of peace
and wholeness, as told in this letter from Kathleen in Utah:

*I had the conscious realization that I had attained enlightenment when I
became forty years old. I had the understanding that the blindness had been
removed from my mind and my spiritual eyes had been opened, which is the
gift of seership. I felt the weight of the world lifted from my shoulders. Life
was no longer a burden of suffering, sorrow, or depression. I felt ten years
younger as I had the feeling that I had found the fountain of youth. I sensed
a beautiful place of peace and wholeness.*

*Then nearly a year later I went through a beautiful and powerful mysti-
cal experience. I was so overwhelmed by the power of God that I felt like
my head was being pushed through a small opening, and I was quickened in
the Spirit . . . and led by revelation to fulfill the mission that I came to earth
to accomplish.*

The conscious realization of Truth can be the experience of everyone as
the angels are freed from ego projection.

The I AM that I AM in the midst of me is omnipotent, all knowing, all seeing, eternally doing and being. This is my Divine Consciousness, the Truth of me.

I am aware of the dynamic energy of this Holy Self going before me, creating according to the highest vision, and revealing the Divine Standard in my life and affairs.

I feel the Divine Radiation. I AM shining abundance. I AM wholeness flowing into perfect expression. I AM the radiation of unconditional love. I AM the light of joy, the beam of happiness, the ray of contentment.

I AM all. Because I AM all, I HAVE all, and I now see the perfect expression of completeness, divine order, and glorious harmony in my life.

I have seen the Truth. My affairs are now an extension of the I AM Self, my Divine Consciousness, and there is nothing more to seek. I am free. I now rest in the Presence of my Holiness.

EIGHT

The Angels Are the Laws of Life

When I was ten I worked for my uncle in a drugstore in Alice, Texas. Finishing up my chores late one afternoon, I walked out of the store and heard a man shout, "Stop in the name of the law!" I froze; I didn't move a muscle—not until a young man raced past me with a deputy sheriff in hot pursuit. I hadn't done anything wrong, but the authority of the law had spoken and I obeyed.

Growing up it seemed that if you did the right thing, you wouldn't get into trouble. The only problem with that philosophy, though, is that what's right and what's not can get a bit fuzzy on the third-dimensional plane. I'm not talking about generally accepted standards of morality here; I'm speaking of the *Law of Reality*—that awesome force that unchains us and lets us be all that we were created to be, without harming others in any way. Just being humanly "good" without understanding the absolute Rightness, Truth, and Power of *Spiritual Law* is not a passport to lasting happiness and fulfillment.

Spiritual Law is the way the universe works. It is energy in action according to a predetermined objective, as in the Law of Wholeness, the Law of Abundance, the Law of Love. It is the Power of God in operation as *Cause*, as *Principle*, as *Truth*. It is the sum total of the Omniscience Energy of the universe saying, "This is the way it is, and nothing can change my mind. You are forever whole and flawless, abundantly supplied with every good thing, experiencing love in every encounter, enjoying success and fulfillment in every activity of life, and remaining eternally in a state of gladness, joy, and contentment. These are inviolable principles upheld by the agents of cosmic law."

The Tibetan master Djwhal Khul has said that divine law "is the motivating, qualified agent of the divine will."[1] Therefore, the twenty-two angels, as agents of the divine will, represent the fullness of the law. Further evidence of this angelic authority is found in ancient wisdom teachings, which identified cosmic law with the twenty-two letters of the Hebrew alphabet: "Here they are known as the twenty-two sounds produced by God to be his ministering angels, established to govern all outer form."[2]

Dr. Emmet Fox, the great metaphysical teacher, once wrote, "Man has dominion over all things when he knows the Law. . . . The Law gives you power to attain prosperity and position without infringing the rights and opportunities of anyone else in the world. . . . The Law gives you Independence so that you can build your own life in your own way, in accordance with your own ideas and ideals. . . . The Law will give you authority over the past as well as the future. *Oh, how I love Thy Law.*"³

The angels within us are "Thy Law"—the very law of our being. And remember that the angels are our inherent powers, which means that the living energies of our consciousness constitute the law of life, the law of our personal worlds.

Joel Goldsmith, author, teacher, and founder of The Infinite Way movement, wrote: "During the day, whether doing housework, driving a car, selling or buying, we must consciously remember that we are the law unto our universe, and that means that we are a law of love unto all with whom we come in contact. We should consciously remember that we do not need anything, because we are the law of supply in action—we can feed 'five thousand' of those who do not yet know their identity."⁴

But when we don't know the Law, or are not consciously aware of the way things really are, we make up our own laws—and then we have to live with them until they are repealed through an understanding that these self-imposed ordinances are in violation of our own inner Supreme Court.

Some of the laws that we have passed include the laws of disease and death, loneliness and unfulfillment, lack and limitation, and a whole range of mandates based on the false idea of suffering. A simple definition of a self-created law is the idea that anything external to us has power over us. When we believe that and follow such a law, we block the healing energy of the angels. For example, if our lives are not whole, it means that we have created a law corresponding to incompletion. If we are afraid of something, whether a particular type of food, person, or condition, we reveal that we have established a rule demanding that we fear that thing and act accordingly or else we will be punished by the very law that we invented.

Isn't it time to get out of the law-making business and rely only on the Constitution of Being, the Original Statutes of God? We are not reaping much happiness from our own laws, and they certainly won't save us from bondage of one form or another. In fact, we have made ourselves puppets and victims by trying to obey our fears and avoid a self-imposed punishment. We set up a law by believing that something is not good for us, but in a moment of weakness we give in. Then we feel guilty, and the ego tells us that all guilt must be punished, so we experience the consequences of "being bad" by having a malfunction of the body or a breakdown in our affairs. Do you see the endless cycle of action-guilt-punishment that this insanity can produce?

Perhaps a spiritual anarchy is necessary to break down the whole due process of law on the inner planes of human consciousness. Our objective would be to take away all control from the ego, which says, "You can't do this or that will happen," and give all authority to the One Government within that says, "Forget your puny laws of ego and dare to live life to the fullest according to the Law of Reality." That's what the angels are waiting for. They represent the eternal verities of life, which will be expressed in our personal worlds when we get the ego out of the way.

How do we break through the ego's projection of misqualified energy and get back in tune with the Law of Reality? One day in a conversation with the Angel of Discernment, I asked that question and was surprised to hear, "*Do not practice echolalia.*" When I asked what the word meant, he said, "*Look it up.*"

The dictionary defines *echolalia* as a condition of "automatic repetition by someone of words spoken in his presence." I began to understand, particularly in reference to the ego. Our lower nature says, "I don't feel so good." And we say, "I don't feel so good." The ego talks limitation, so we talk limitation. The ego speaks of futility and unfulfillment, and so do we. No wonder that echolalia is considered a mental disorder.

So I asked the angel, "How do we cure ourselves of this malady and siphon off some of that ego energy?"

"*Break the rule of listening to solar plexus chatter that says you are less than you are, and stop repeating the lies emanating from below. Listen to your heart and accept the fullness of yourself.*"

I got it.

While we were talking about breaking rules in order to adhere to cosmic law, four others angels joined us: the Angel of Order and Harmony, the Angel of Imagination and Liberation, the Angel of Spiritual Understanding, and the Angel of Loving Relationships. We talked for over an hour on how to work on "the right side of the law"—the side of the angels—each one contributing to the conversation. From this very personal experience of seeing how to neutralize the ego from their perspective, I wrote an article for *The Quartus Report*, the newsletter for the Quartus Foundation. Based on the input of the angels, my goal was to inspire people to stretch their minds, express their feelings, and enjoy life by taking the little child out of the closet—because that's what I was going to do. Here's the gist of the article.

Rule to be broken: The one that says fantasies are unreal
and just make-believe, and must be suppressed—particularly
if there is a connotation of being a little too free and frisky.
Let's take a day, a week, or a month and play
"dreamcastle." Let's get a notebook and live with it for a
period of time, writing down everything we can see
ourselves doing in our wildest imagination—without any
limitations whatsoever.

You say you're in your nineties and have always
dreamed about bicycling through the French countryside
with the perfect companion, but now you are too old. Write
it down anyway. You may be surprised what the Universe

has in store for you in line with the Principle of Joy, once you stretch your mind with feeling.

You may want to paint, write a book, or play an instrument, but you don't have the time, talent, or money to try. Excuses. Play the game and see what happens. Throw away every idea of restriction and limitation having to do with age, finances, education, and seeming responsibilities. See yourself living the way you want to live, having the things you want to have, doing what you want to do in the grandest scale imaginable—and make it fun. What you're doing in the process is telling the ego that you're not confined to its idea of straightjacket living, thereby getting more in tune with the heavenly ordinance of happiness and the holy standard of bliss.

The Angel of Imagination and Liberation had said that "when you reach for the distant stars in your imagination, you expand the tent of consciousness— and in doing so, you touch the realm of present possibilities that has already been manifest according to your present state of consciousness, but of which you were unaware." That seems to be the purpose of the dreamcastle game.

Rule to be broken: The one that says we must place restrictions on how we express our feelings. Men are told not to cry, that it's unmanly . . . to be careful in expressing love to another man, that it may imply something other than simple affection . . . to be on guard in relating to women, that tenderness, warmth, and loving attention can be misconstrued as a sexual advance. And women are warned against being too bold, too powerful, too audacious, too strong—or the opposite of all of the above.

We are so caught up in being "correct" that we don't know how to handle our feelings. And so we repress them, but when they come back up, they arise as ego-thoughts that make us feel even less than human, which again shuts out the shining light of the radiant Truth of Being. Remember the Law of the Angel of Loving Relationships: "You will experience only deep, abiding love in each encounter with every form of life, for love is the governing principle of all that exists."

Rule to be broken: Forget about the sensuous pleasure of life. Sensuous means seeking that which is delicious, exquisite, and enjoyable—which is something we may try to rise above when we embark on the spiritual journey. But when those greatly appealing things are "beneath" us, we're saying that we know more what's best for us than the original Laws of Being. And the radiant energy of the laws of joy, fulfillment, and all that is delightful in life is screened out even more.

Rule to be broken: What we really want to do in life may not be right for us, or will disappoint family and friends, or isn't conducive to spiritual growth. We break that rule and look to the Angelic Law that says, "Take courage and be thyself!"

When we repress our dreams, the shadow of those dreams will surface later with energy loaded with anger and hostility. Also, if we always do, say, and act in accordance with what other people think and expect of us, we're not being ourselves. We're hiding our child in the closet—the one who wants to kick up his or her heels and live! And when we finally let the child out, what we see is a monster.

Do you see what can happen when we follow our heart and decide to be who we are, rather than a certain image to protect? We are neutralizing the ego who says, "Dreams are a waste of time . . . you can never be really free . . . pleasure is sinful . . . you can't do that, people will get the wrong idea . . . don't do what you want to do because your family won't approve . . . etc."

The higher we soar in consciousness, the greater the separation from the ego. And the greater the separation, the greater the connection with the Supreme Decrees of the Divine Principles. Of course, we have to be discerning in our flight to freedom, but that energy is an integral part of us as the Angel of Discernment, and we can be sure that he will provide us with all the navigational skills we'll need for the journey.

Let's work with the angels and get on the right side of the law. When we do, we won't have so many "rules" to follow. Isn't that what freedom means?

A month after the article appeared, I received a letter from Glen in Colorado. He wrote:

"Pent up" would be the best way to describe how I have lived most of my life . . . holding back what I really wanted to do for fear of alienating my mother, losing my wife, and getting fired from my job. Because I was so dissatisfied with everything, all of that was probably going to happen anyway. But what you wrote made me think that everything didn't have to be a dead end, that maybe I could follow my heart.

I've also read your Angel *book, so I decided to play dreamcastles with the Angel of Imagination. She kept pushing me, like "You don't reach very high, do you?" and "Is that all you can see?" After a couple of days I got the hang of it and went kind of crazy in my imagination. I was on a worldwide tour with this group, playing the guitar and singing, and everywhere we went the stadiums were packed for our performances—and record sales were in the tens of millions.*

I felt kind of childish playing the game, but I got a lot of inner satisfaction. Then about a month later I got a phone call from a high school buddy who asked me if I would consider trying out for his band—he's pretty well known in this area, but I hadn't seen him in over ten years. He knew I'd played the guitar back in school and had heard that I'd gotten pretty good at it.

To make a long story short, I'm not on a worldwide tour yet, but neither am I selling insurance. A happy pastime has become a happy career, and even my wife and mother have come around. Diana (the Angel of Imagination and Liberation) and I see each other regularly now."

I wonder what will happen when his other twenty-one angels are freed to soar to their greatest heights.

> *Divine Laws are the Principles of Being, the living energies of the angels, the realities of life, the way things are in Truth.*
>
> *The Law says my body is whole, vibrant, and well—that radiant health is my true nature. Regardless of appearances, I accept this Truth.*
>
> *The Law says that scarcity is against the Law, that abundance is natural, and that my finances are continually in a state of all-sufficiency. Regardless of appearances, I accept this Truth.*
>
> *The Law says my relationships are warm, loving, caring, and meaningful, and that everyone I meet reflects back to me the true spirit of love and goodwill. Regardless of appearances, I accept this Truth.*

The Law says my success in life is assured, that I am in my true place doing what I love, and loving what I do. Regardless of appearances, I accept this Truth.

The Law says that what I accept, I will experience. I have accepted with all my heart and mind, and I know that by Law, all that is good, true, and beautiful in life is rushing to me now. The Law is fulfilled, and so am I.

NINE

The Angels and Right Livelihood

I have often thought of "right livelihood" as doing what you love, and loving what you do—and getting paid for it. This could be another way of defining success, which would mean that in the world at large, the truly successful people are in a distinct minority. How many people do you know who can hardly wait to get out of bed in the mornings and go to work? Very few. Perhaps it's because they are trying to make a living instead of a life and have blocked that radiant energy of fulfillment and achievement—the Angel of Success.

Everyone has a divine purpose relating to right livelihood that may have been communicated since childhood in the form of special interests, hidden yearnings, and "heart's desires." What we have wanted to do or be usually reflects certain talents and abilities that we came in with, but we may have discounted a particular gift if we could not see it as a means of supporting ourselves—or because the timing wasn't right.

The Angel of Success once asked me to remember what I had always wanted to do. I said, "Write a book." I recalled my secret writings as a young boy, my love of books, and later my fascination with classical literature and the works of the great philosophers. "But I never considered the idea of writing books as a career," I said.

"*In another life you wrote many books,*" said the angel, "*but you did not achieve the degree of literary success that you sought. The thought of rejection has continued in your lower mind, which inhibited you in this life; thus the necessity of transferring your skills into related fields until you were ready to commence your true work.*"

"I just wish I hadn't waited so long."

"*You were equating success with a ladder which you felt you had to climb, yet each level reached revealed only further dissatisfaction. It was this discontent that eventually led you to the writing of the first book. There was no waste of time or effort in the preceding years, however, for you were being prepared for what was to come. And time is never lost, for I am its master. You will fulfill your purpose for being.*"

———

The voice heard by a woman in Kansas also revealed that her life up to the present moment had been a preparation for what is ahead.

Right after talking to you I went out in the car and drove around. Many times when I do this, and the conscious mind is busily engaged in driving, thoughts or intuitive things come to me. But I marked yesterday down on my calendar because it was the most eventful message I have ever received in my life. I heard a different voice, one that I have not heard before. It was so profound that I had to stop the car. It was not in the least frightening, but very reassuring.

I was told enough to fill volumes of books in just a few fleeting seconds. I was shown how my whole life so far has led up to this point, what my true function in this life is, and how the future will be for me if I do this work. I guess you would call it direct revelation . . . and I know exactly what I'm supposed to do now.

Another letter, this one from Caroline in Washington, tells about the appearance of an angel, a dramatic heightening of intuitive abilities, and a change in consciousness, all in preparation for a new career of service to others.

Early one summer morning in 1985, when I was working in a holistic medical clinic, a vision appeared to me that would change my life forever.

I had come in early to the clinic to prepare homeopathic medicines for the patients. As I sat with a row of bottles in front of me, I started to feel a warm, tingling feeling that I experience in deep mediation. I looked up from my work and saw before me a bright, radiant light. Through this pulsating light appeared the figure of an angel. I stared at the figure and she stared back at me with a loving countenance that beckoned me to feel no fear. I was awestruck. The whole room was consumed with light and love.

I could hear her words inside my head: "Behold the angel . . . will you do my work?"

I responded "yes" in my heart but my lips could not move; I was speechless. Her radiant, iridescent, quivering wings seemed to reach out to me and to enfold me. I couldn't believe what I was seeing and wished I was not alone in this experience. I was filled with awe and gratitude. After I had acknowledged her presence and had affirmed that I would certainly be honored to do whatever work was required, the light began to dim and my angel stepped back into her world.

I remember being absolutely stunned and unable to move for a long time. Then I got up and something prompted me to go over to a large bunch of flowers sitting on the reception desk. I was led to look into the flowers and put my ear up to them. I could hear beautiful music coming from them like little flutes made from reeds. I was in a heightened state, aware of everything on all levels at once. It was wonderful. The whole experience lasted a few minutes, but it felt like a lifetime.

I wondered what I was supposed to do. And who was I to have a direct experience with an angel? I pondered this in my heart and allowed myself to readjust to my surroundings. At that point, the doctor and the patients began to enter the office. It was 8 A.M. I felt elated and intuitive. I wanted to discuss this with someone but could tell no one. From that moment (and I still have this gift) I could tell intuitively what was wrong with the patients. I knew the emotional cause of their illness; I knew what medicines were needed for treatment, what the dosage would be, and how long it would take to effect a cure. I also felt a direct connection with each person.

I stayed in this exalted, elevated state for about ten days, and everything around me had meaning. I decided then that the meaning of the words spoken by the angel—"Will you do my work?"—meant that I must become more like an angel in my life, that I needed to change from being critical and judgmental to being loving, kind, and understanding. I took this message as a challenge for me to clean up my life and surrender to my purpose. From that moment on in 1985, I was guided continually to be the gentle, loving voice of God's angel in my life.

Then, after two years of preparation, I was given my real purpose—to create an angel doll and therapeutic audiotapes to help children in need. So, without any particular training or knowledge, I proceeded. I listened everyday in my meditations to the wisdom and guidance of my angel, and everything that I have needed for this project has been brought to me. Now, seven years later, the angel dolls and tapes are selling well, and have brought miraculous healings to many children who have them.

Charles Fillmore, cofounder of the Unity movement, defines success as "attainment of a desired goal. Success comes as the result of faithfulness and earnestness in the application of God's Law."[1]

To apply the law, we must be consciously aware that there is a living, intelligent, energy within us, an angel who knows the Holy Self's plan and purpose and who will help us structure our lives for maximum achievement. When we begin to work with this angel, we quickly find our true place and discover that we have all the tools necessary to build a highly successful lifework.

As Earl in California wrote:

I started working with the Saturn energy (the Angel of Success) *in the fall of 1993, after reading your book—mostly because I didn't know what I wanted to do for the rest of my life. It wasn't that I was a failure. I was doing okay financially, but something was gnawing at me. I thought that maybe it was because I couldn't see myself selling real estate forever, regardless of the money I made, and that there was something else I should be doing. So when I made contact with Saturn, he asked me to look ahead five years and tell him what I saw.*

After a few minutes, and somewhat shocked because of the clearness of the vision, I said, "An unfulfilled, loud, boorish heavy drinker, trying to pressure people into buying homes they can't afford just to get the commission." What amazed me was that I drink very little now, I consider myself as fairly urbane with a soft sales approach, and I've really never been afraid of the future.

He said, "You have seen where you are headed—a personality and lifestyle predicated on fear." When I asked him what I should do, he said, "Look at this picture." It was a color photograph of me standing on a stage talking. I knew it was a church, and the people in the audience were my congregation. I've been studying metaphysics for ten years, but the idea of being a minister has never entered my mind. Not until now, and it seems right. Saturn knew what I was supposed to be doing all along.

In 1994 this man began taking the necessary courses to become a New Thought minister.

Not everyone is in a preparatory stage for future fulfillment. Some may be so out of sync with the idea of right livelihood that the search for another job should begin at once. Look at the work you're involved in and consider that you may be exactly where you're supposed to be at this time in your life for great joy and fulfillment. The discouragement and sense of futility could simply be an indication that you have not recognized the Principle of Success abiding within you—that pulsating thought form of pure energy that knows itself as the power to achieve anything worthwhile in life, right where you are.

When Frank in Georgia discovered the Angel of Success, he immediately thought of quitting his job and forming his own company for greater freedom and opportunity. He said:

I had even written my letter of resignation, but before I could submit it, I heard, "Wait. Explore the possibilities here. Ask about the planned expansion and your role in the new organization."

I went to my boss the next morning and said that "my intuition tells me that something is going on behind the scenes, and I'd like to know how it's going to affect me." He looked surprised and said that my gut feeling was right on—that a merger with another firm was in the works, that it was all very confidential now, but that I was being looked at to head up one of the new divisions.

That was six months ago. Now I've got my cake and I'm eating it too, because it's like running my own company but with all the perks of a long-established organization. And I've never been happier with my work. I owe the Angel of Success a debt of gratitude.

Whether the seeds of magnificent success are to be found right where we're standing or are waiting to sprout on a distant horizon, it is all in keeping with our Soul's purpose. Based on letters received from and conversations I've had with people over the past decade—and from my own experiences—I've come to the conclusion that right livelihood and true place success are in direct relationship to our willingness to surrender to that purpose. What this means is consenting to be employed by the Master within, the Essential Self. Let's take another look at that Divine Person and get a feel for what It has in mind.

Our Reality is a living, Self-conscious Entity who is all-wise, all-knowing, all-loving, infinitely creative, and possessing the fullness of the attributes of Supreme Being. This Eternal Self is the one who motivates the human consciousness into incarnation, impulsing, directing the male-female choice; the choice of parents for what they can contribute to the physical life experience of the personality; the kind of physical, emotional, and mental vehicles that will be utilized; and the particularly unique system of planetary (astrological) energies under which the person will incarnate. The Self also determines when it is time to drop the physical body and return home, which is usually at the point at which the Self sees that no further progress can be made in fulfilling Its purpose.

Everything is planned by the Self to accelerate the evolutionary process of individual consciousness, leading ultimately to the final fusion of Self and personality. With each incarnation of consciousness, the Self has a purpose, an intention for maximum Self-fulfillment, which involves the personality as a channel for that expression. When we agree to be that channel, the doors to the angels are opened, and we find true success in our world.

Gloria in New York told me that when she finally committed "to be used" by the Master Self in fulfilling Its purpose, her whole life was dramatically turned around in a matter of days. She said:

I had not been able to work with the angels—no words or visions, not even intuitive feelings—until I made the conscious decision to serve only the Christ within. Shortly after that I began to see, with my mind, little globes of light. I said, "I choose to be a success for Christ's sake," and one of the globes grew larger and brighter. I knew this was the Angel of Success. And I said, "Let the divine purpose for me be manifest now."

Three days later I had a telephone call from someone I hadn't heard from in years. This not only led to a new career in fashion design but also to a partnership with a man who puts God first in life, the man I soon will marry. The word "success" means so many things . . . it is the achievement of all that's good in life.

Early one morning, while I was conversing with the Angel of Success on the idea of working solely for the Chief Executive within, he said, *"There cannot be true success without love."* When I asked him to explain what he meant, he suggested that the Angel of Unconditional Love and Freedom join us.

I repeated the question to the Love angel and received the following message.

Understand that everything is the essence, energy, substance of God, all of which is love. Anything that could possibly happen to anyone on this planet—whether the happening is considered "good" or "bad"—is the result of how the energy of love was used. Love is the greatest power in the universe. In fact, it is the only Power. All other powers, energies, forces, and laws are derived from this one creating, sustaining, maintaining power that permeates and embraces all that is. And in every activity of life, you are either honoring it or transgressing it.

If the energy of love is adulterated in any way through thought, word, or action, the pollution returns to you as a negative life experience. If you uphold this power, the return is positive. If you see anything less or other than the Holy Self in others, even if you are judging another's humanness, you are transgressing the law of love because all judgment of others is a self-directed judgment, a self-condemnation that will return in kind.

Example: You perceive that someone is ill, out of work, or experiencing financial lack. If you judge by appearances and accept that judgment, you are restricting the flow of the energies of wholeness, success, and abundance within to the degree of the judgment. And the result will be less vitality, achievement, and prosperity in your life. There is only one Self, and to judge another is to pass sentence on yourself.

I understood then, perhaps more than I ever had, that Love is indeed the essential quality of all that is, and I was reminded of a story told by a friend of mine. He had been terribly dissatisfied in his job, so much so that he sought help from a spiritual counselor. The counselor told him that he could not find advancement and fulfillment in his career until he could first truly love what he was doing in his present position. When my friend asked how to do that, he was told to find someone in the company who loved his or her work and understand why. He found that person, and learned the lesson that we always have a choice—that we can choose to be happy where we are, regardless of the circumstances surrounding us.

My friend began to pour love into his work, to make everything a joyful adventure of doing his best and looking for only the good in every situation. In less than two months he was not only given a promotion within his company but was also offered a position at another firm. He had found that love is truly the motivating power of success in life.

I'm sure that Peggy in California would vouch for that, for her love of angels and animals has led her into a successful new enterprise called Angel'ings.

Peggy wrote me in the summer of 1994, saying that

While unemployed and striving to get my life in order, I began cocreat-

ing a series of angel image cards. I didn't have the funds to have them printed, yet the urge to create them continued to inspire me forward. Then someone loaned me the money and they were printed, and I began to sell them to local stores.

One day while visiting my oldest daughter's ceramic store, I was inspired to add wings to small animals—thus, Angel'ings came into being. Angel'ings are the guardian angels of the animals of Mother Earth. They are here to remind us that all creatures are in our care.

Later, in chatting with someone who had purchased one of my angel cards, I mentioned the Angel'ings. When she offered financial aid, I was incredibly moved—I felt the angels were truly blessing and supporting us. We began production, and six weeks later we were accepted into a very exclusive gift catalog. Then we had to move because my daughter's store is too small for production—and we found the perfect building. The angels are truly our working partners.

The angels can also be "working partners" for an established business that needs an infusion of success energy. In his book *Creative Mind and Success*, Ernest Holmes wrote, "If you are . . . not doing good business, look carefully into your own thought and see what you will find. You will find that it is an established belief there that business is not good. You are not feeling a sense of activity. You will not find within your thought any feeling of success. You are not expecting many customers."

Holmes continued: "Now, what are you going to do about it? This is what you must do. For every time that you have thought failure you are going to replace it with strong radiant thoughts of success." (*This frees the Angel of Success.*) "You are going to speak activity into your business." (*The Angel of the Creative Word goes to work.*) "You are going daily to see nothing but activity and to know that it is Law that you are using, Universal Law, and as such your thought is as sure as the thought of God." (*This right seeing is the way of the Angel of Imagination and Liberation.*)

"You will see only what you desire and in the silence of your soul you will speak and it will be done unto you. You will come to believe that a great Divine Love flows through you and your affairs."[2]

Holmes's advice is similar to that given to Sydney in Houston by the Angel of Success:

The angel took the form of a large man with a long, flowing beard and long gray hair, much like Michelangelo's sculpture of Moses. I asked him what I needed to do to remove any ego projections from his energy. Immediately the Angel of Imagination appeared beside him, and Success said, "You need to use her to imagine your True Success just as you want it." Then he brought in the Angel of Unconditional Love and Freedom and said, "You need to use him to love your self more, and to love all others unconditionally. Drop all judgments of everything."

I promised I would do both. Then I asked him what he wanted me to give him, and he said, "Your watch, your sense of time. Do not judge the outpicturing of your success in the sense of time. Let me take care of that. You need only imagine your success, follow the steps, and don't worry about the time it takes to manifest your dreams."

This magic is unending.

Melanie of Oklahoma City was told by the Angel of Success that she was "indispensable." She said:

I couldn't really understand this because I own a small business, and have never considered myself indispensable to anything.

The angel was right; each one of us is indispensable. Regardless of what we do in life to earn a living, we all hold a piece of the planetary puzzle. In ecology we see that every species is vital to the living chain, that the whole is not complete without all of its parts. This is also true of the living chain of humanity.

In the universal scheme of things, you are as important as any king, queen, head of state, or elected official—and you do make a difference, a crucial difference. You are a mind, a state of consciousness that is linked in the invisible energies with every other individual on the face of the earth and beyond. And without your connection in this mind-link, the entire chain would fall apart.

So you are not only important to the world, you are indeed *indispensable*. Keep that in mind the next time you think that "little me" can't make a meaningful contribution. You already are, simply by being an essential part of the whole. With this understanding, a shift in consciousness takes place that enables the Angel of Success to lead you into right livelihood. It happens when you realize that you are necessary, that you are needed in this world. Acceptance of that truth opens new doors for you and places you on a direct line toward your true place in life.

I came into this world with a very specific purpose.

   I came to fulfill a mission.

   I came to love life and realize the truth about me.

   I came to contribute to this world.

   I am a part of God and the fullness of the Godhead dwells in me. In the Mind of God, no one, or no thing, is useless or meaningless. Everyone and everything is of critical importance to the balance and order of the universe. Without me, God would not be complete. Without me, the universe would lose its equilibrium.

   All that is before me to do, I do with happy enthusiasm, for nothing is too insignificant. And never again will there be a sense of futility in my life.

   I am overflowing with gratitude to God for the opportunity to be in physical form at this time. I am thankful to be right where I am, right now, serving all who come my way with love, joy, understanding, and forgiveness.

   Recognizing my true worth, I now go forth with uplifted vision. I see with the inner eye the loving and prospering activity of the Holy Self within. I see with my physical eyes lavish abundance everywhere. I am peaceful, powerful, and poised, for I know who I am.

TEN

The Angels and Prosperity

In order to understand that unlimited abundance is a natural part of life on the third-dimensional plane, we must accept the fact that God is fully manifest as each individual being. We are the Allness of God in unique expression, and in the individualizing process, nothing was left out. The manifestation was, and is, complete. Right at this moment, regardless of seeming circumstances, the lavish wealth of the universe is within us, ready to flow out into visibility through our conscious awareness of its instant availability.

Whenever we experience a shortage of money, it means that we are registering a sense of *want*—a feeling of incompletion—rather than a realization of *have*. How strange this is. We have been given everything, and the kingdom within is bulging with awesome abundance, yet we see scarcity, which is a direct denial of our true nature. No wonder that Emerson said that "wealth is moral . . . the only sin is limitation."[1] Sin means "falling short of the divine law"[2]—and we certainly do place ourselves outside the law of abundance when we fail to acknowledge that we are that principle in action.

The I AM of us, our Essential Self, is conscious of money as a spiritual idea and knows that we require this medium of exchange while in physical form. In order for this infinite supply to flow from center to circumference and out into the phenomenal world to appear as energy-in-form, the Spirit-Self indwelling extended a dynamic thought form into our mental-emotional system: *the Power to be conscious of abundance*, a living, intelligent sphere of energy that knows Itself as unlimited riches. This is the Angel of Abundance. When we are consciously aware of this angel and her continuously flowing fountain of prosperity, we bring her power into our minds and hearts, and the channel between the invisible and visible worlds is complete.

Several years ago we were given the opportunity to prove the principle of all-sufficiency. During one particular month, expenses exceeded income by about $3,000. Jan and I were not familiar with the angels within at that time, but we knew that the Source of our prosperity was individualized as the Reality of our being, and that there was a pocket of energy within our force fields that corresponded to financial well-being. Knowing that a consciousness of abundance is the law of supply in action, we began contemplating that energy, and drew it into our conscious awareness to radiate through us. Without realizing it, we were actually working with the "Hand of God" responsible for material prosperity.

When the bank statement came at the end of the month, there was an additional $3,500 in the account. We went back over the checks and deposits in previous statements and couldn't figure out how the money was credited to us. Wondering if the bank had made an error, we called and told them about the sudden increase in our account. They called back later to say that their records reflected no error on their part and that the money was ours. To this day we have no logical explanation for this multiplication of provisions—except we know now that angels do work in mysterious ways.

Elisha in Greece would concur, with a few cosmic giggles added for flavor. Here's her story:

For many years I have been living out of the pockets of the Universe. When I needed money, I would order it from the hilltop behind my house where a small hidden cave provided shelter from the elements and an inspiring view of great beauty. Whenever I would call for money, it would come my way, either by someone asking me for paid help in home, field, vineyard, or olive grove, or by surprise donations arriving in the mail within three days. On one occasion, however, timing and cosmic humor hit a record.

I had gone up to my cave early one morning, had opened to the king-

dom within and invited the Angel of Abundance to come forth. I profoundly thanked my Holy Source for everything I had and was, and stated that I now needed money so that I could continue to live with ease and grace in my third-dimensional world. I called forth, "Money, money, money!" And I saw it before me, bills and golden coins dancing happily round and round with me.

Being part of the Universe, everything I do is known by it, and every call I make is heard by my Source, just as I hear Its call. So I thanked my Holy Source for having heard and answered my need, then stood up and began the descent. How light I felt on the rocky path, how brilliantly alive the world around me was in the morning sun! Deciding to take a little detour, I followed the pathway to my vineyard, but oh, what a sight appeared before me. There, engrossed in single-minded relish, stood my neighbor's goat, tethered on a rope that reached halfway into my vineyard!

I yelled, "How dare you, animal! Git ye out at once!" During a whole night's grazing she had eaten all the leaves within the range of her rope, and bunches of grapes dangled from the bare vines. As I shortened her rope to a safe length from my vineyard, my dismay gave way to a sense of great inner calm. There was this beautiful goat standing before me, just looking at me with her golden eyes. I scratched her behind her horns and decided to wait there for her owner to come. He had not milked her and would arrive soon.

I was thinking about how long it would take for new leaves to grow, slowing down the ripening process of the grapes, when I heard my neighbor's cheerful voice. "Well, a bright and early good morning to you!"

he said. "And to you too," I responded. Then he saw the rope and my vineyard.

"Oh my," he said. "I guess I didn't check the rope when I tethered her last night. I am sorry about it. You won't report it, will you?" Before I could answer, he added quickly, "How much do I owe you? How much do you want in recompense?"

I had not counted the number of affected vines, let alone their monetary value, but my mouth said, "Five thousand drachmas."

My neighbor said, "All right. Come to my shop in town and collect it."

I did not show my surprise at the high sum of money I had asked for, nor my neighbor's unquestioning acceptance of the deal. I agreed and we shook hands, and I continued on my way down the hill to my house, full of cosmic giggles rippling through me. I thought, oh my beloved Angel of Abundance . . . this sure has been the most fun way you have responded to my call!

Beverly in Michigan had an interesting teaching experience from the Angel of Abundance. When she tapped into that energy, she heard:

"Beverly, all the abundance that God knows, and all the abundance that God has in the Kingdom, is yours. It is all yours, now! And it has been within you for you to use and enjoy right from your very beginning.

"I have been calling you and calling you, but the door has been closed from your side and you've been leaning so hard against it. You've been looking away in the opposite direction from me, trying to find your good, trying to find abundance and fulfillment out there, when right within you, your God-Self is overflowing with every kind of abundance.

"I think you're beginning to get it. I can see that the door is opening a crack and you're growing weary of searching out there for some little crumbs of contentment, which are sometimes snapped up by the birds before you can gather them in to ease the emptiness you feel.

"You are discovering that all the prayers and affirmations in the world that cry and flow out of neediness can only breed more sense of neediness and attract more emptiness to manifest in your experience. The Way to your good is singing hymns of gratitude . . . gratitude is The Way and the Order of the day, because gratitude is acceptance. Your gratitude is your accepting your inheritance. Your gratitude is your trusting in the givingness of your Father. Accepting and trusting, and yes, surrendering with all your heart and all your mind is what has opened the door to the treasure house within."

By now I felt as though I were lying back and floating upon the sustaining Infinite. The Angel of Abundance had called and the connection was open and clear, and I stood in the Light of Understanding. However, the angel wasn't through with the lesson yet. As I lay basking in the warm light and feeling overwhelming gratitude for the wonder and great simplicity of the Universal Plan, the angel prodded me into alertness by explaining another phase of the Truth.

"Beverly, you must see and understand the picture that I will draw for you. God is not person! I want you to get that once and for all. God is not person—God is Impersonal Energy, and all is energy, only energy. Can you conceive of the magnitude of this idea?

"*Be silent and feel the energy all around you, within you, above you, beneath your feet—holding you as gravity to the Earth, yet allowing you to soar to the heights of heaven. Feel this imponderable energy stretching into Infinity, attracting to you all the wonders you have accepted.*

"*Now I'm going to draw a picture for you using an example that you are sure to understand. Since you are well versed in gardening, you know full well that the tiny mustard seed, the petunia, and the beautiful rose are all endowed within each one individually to fulfill its own identity. Now, if you plant petunias, you had better not expect to get roses, because the Law says that if you plant petunias, you're going to get petunias!*

"*Beverly, even though the seeds contain the energy and the potential design program to become beautiful flowers, you know that they must be taken out of the packet and planted in the most fertile soil that you can prepare. You see, the seed is like an idea, a desire, an urge to grow, to become, that must be planted in a fertile consciousness in order to come into flowering fruition.*

"*As a prudent gardener, you also know that as you drop the pregnant seed into the fertile soil, you let go of the whole unseen process and you release this stage of development into the Universe. The Universe knows and supplies all that is needed. In other words, you trust the divine process, knowing that this unseen stage is being perfectly orchestrated and cultivated by divine energy. You forgo any urge to dig into the developing garden to see what's happening and how well things are progressing, and you simply accept and trust and await the certain manifestation of abundant beauty.*

"All of this you know. Now, let's go back to impersonal God-Energy. God-Energy IS. It just IS, and the will of this God-Energy is the urge to express Itself. This is the manifestation process. This God-Energy is impersonal, therefore. It never gets into judgment, never gets into whether we deserve to see Its manifestation, or if we are worthy or unworthy, saint or sinner. This judgment business is always the business of ego. Remember that the energy of the sun shines on the saint and the sinner alike. The urge of the sun is simply to express itself, to let its light shine forth.

"You see now that your abundance doesn't depend on being worthy or deserving—your abundance is not a reward. Your abundance is the perfect impersonal law of givingness. It is the will of the Father, the urge of God-Energy to express Itself, to give Itself to its beloved individual manifestations. Open yourself to this powerful flow of infinite energy.

"Forever hold this in remembrance: In order for your all-embracing abundance to come to you, it must come through you! Remember your seed sown in fertile soil. It produced blooming magnificence! The impersonal energy manifested through the enriched soil. A seed dropped into a crack in the concrete will also produce and manifest itself as its recognizable design; however, it will be sparse and may not flourish. Ideas and desires potentially starting out as grand ideas, but that pass through and are shaped and undernourished by our own concretized, miscreated belief systems, will always manifest as misshapen, impoverished experiences.

"If you don't get anything else, Beverly, let go of the concretized belief systems, release the fears and anxieties, and open the door. Break open the

crack in the concrete and accept and trust the rich, fertile, infinite God-Energy that urgently desires to give Itself to you. God loves Its expression. Its expression is you!"

Thank you, Angel of Abundance. I am now at peace and living in abundance as the heiress of the kingdom that I truly am.

In conversations with the Venus energy of abundance and with people from coast to coast, I've come to understand that we all have placed restrictions on our prosperity. Harboring resentment toward people who are wealthy; being at odds with our children for not fulfilling our high expectations; claiming to want prosperity but maintaining a comfort zone in a near-poverty level and refusing to do anything to expand our consciousness; condemning materiality; experiencing guilt relating to sexual indiscretions or frustration stemming from sexual problems (money and sex come from the same energy); being critical of others' success—the list is essentially endless, and each one of us has our own "bogey man" in the basement which must be eliminated in consciousness before we can truly enjoy the riches of life.

Simon in Tennessee was reminded of that in a conversation with the Angel of Success.

As the Angel of Success sat at a table across from me dressed in striped trousers, a black swallowtail coat, and a silk top hat, I asked him about Venus, the Angel of Abundance.

He said, "We've been friends within you, but you have work to do before we can be intimate. You must clean out your basement area—there are so many conflicting patterns there that our ability to guide you is impaired. Clean up, toss out, and organize it!"

Venus approached from the left, and I stood to greet her. She had long, wavy blond hair and was wearing a flowing pink dress with diamonds and gold jewelry. She smiled at me, then sat down and held hands with the Angel of Success.

She said, "You must, as you so sagely counseled another, make your own forgiveness list, big and colorful and bright. Clear out your psyche as you clear out unneeded possessions. Then my friend Chronos (Angel of Success) can have integration with you."

I saw a mental picture of us melding into one, and she nodded, saying, "We will then be freed to operate as one in your life."

Holly in New York wrote that the Angel of Abundance appeared to her with handcuffs on her wrists and a gag in her mouth. When she asked the angel to explain the reason for this appearance, the angel said:

"You have bound and gagged me with your drivel."

I had to look the word up to make sure I understood the meaning. It was "foolish and senseless talk; babbling." Then I asked the angel to show me some examples of this behavior.

She said, "You are always rambling on about the state of the economy, the man in the White House, poverty worldwide, and how governments are making beggars of us all. When I try to tell you that you are destabilizing your own inner economy with such talk, you suppress me. And when I attempt to reach through you to offer a helping hand to others, you tie me up with your selfishness. I can release more abundance into your life than you can possibly imagine if you will see me in each person, place, and situation. I am the wealth within everyone and everything, and if you cannot see me in others, you will not see me in yourself. And to give to another is but a transfer of my wealth without diminishing the flow or taking anything away from yourself."

Since then I have let her have her way with me, and with the assistance of the Angel of the Creative Word, I've watched my tongue. Immediately my finances improved, and I'm just getting started.

After *The Angels Within Us* was published, I was reading the chapter on the Angel of Abundance when a series of "flow-throughs" began. The first line of thought was *"What are your intentions regarding money?"* This was followed by *"You should know, because intentions channel energy into expression, and this is the first step in the creative process. The second step is to determine the spiritual purpose on which the intention is based, and step number three is to identify the appropriate energy—that which I am."*

"Is this the Angel of Abundance speaking?" As I asked this question, the angel appeared in mind with a black halter and long multicolored skirt, a brunette beauty with flashing eyes.

"None other. Now, understand that intentions mean what you intend to do, be, and have in life from your highest vision. The spiritual purpose is the divine motive that brings my energy into form. What are your intentions?"

I thought for a moment and said, "To release into manifestation the abundance that I already am and have."

She asked, *"What is your spiritual purpose?"* When I didn't answer right away, she said, *"Try this: My spiritual purpose is to have divine order in my financial affairs, to maintain goodwill with all people and establishments that have given me their trust, and to provide loving service to others in my work of spiritual research and communications. Does that fit with you?"*

"It certainly does!"

"Report this conversation in your journal, keeping in mind that it is MY energy that will produce the manifestation."

I followed her instructions, then added this statement: "With love in my heart, and in the spirit of divine order, goodwill, and loving service, I now remove the restrictions that I have placed on the Energy of Money, and I let it flow easily and naturally throughout my world."

Within a short time, a substantial amount of money from an unexpected source was received.

If you wish to follow this example, keep in mind that you do not have to tell the angel about your personal needs or what to do. You simply provide the clear channel by lifting all restrictions on her energy, and she will carry out her own plan of adhering to divine principle.

In a recent conversation with the Angel of Abundance, I was told that *"lasting material riches must come forth from inner spiritual riches. There is no other way."* To me, this meant being consciously aware of the abounding treasures of the kingdom within—that pulsating energy of bounty and wealth, the very spirit of infinite plenty indwelling—and feeling-knowing-being spiritually rich, moment by moment, day by day. The richness of consciousness will then go before us to express as visible supply in the most appropriate manner.

This causal power of prosperity also reminded me that money is energy, and that it is drawn particularly to those who appreciate beauty, quality, order, and harmony. When I asked why, the Angel of Abundance said:

"This energy is of royal origin, born of love and ripened in the kingdom of grace and beauty, and is attracted to an individual who represents a close affinity with that vibration. There are exceptions, but in the long term, one who is slovenly repels the energy, while a loving and noble character evokes it. A person's bearing, especially when warmed with deep unconditional love and a spirit of goodwill, is a crucial attribute in the attraction of financial supply."

Consciousness is indeed the key to a life more abundant, not so much a "prosperity consciousness," but an awareness and understanding that the Allness of the Universe resides within and is forever seeking an outlet through us. We release the Allness through our uplifted consciousness, and it will return to us in the fullness of visible form according to our power of attraction. And the beacon light is love.

My conscious awareness of the Divine Presence within me as my supply is my supply. I am now consciously aware of this indwelling fountain of overflowing abundance. Therefore, I AM abundant supply. My consciousness is the very energy of money.

I am the Spirit of Infinite Plenty individualized. I am boundless abundance, and with love in my heart, I let the universal riches stream forth into perfect manifestation.

What is expressed in love must be returned in full measure. Therefore, wave after wave of visible money supply flows to me now. I am wonderfully rich in consciousness, and I am bountifully supplied with money. I now realize my plan for abundant living.

I see my bank account always filled with an all-sufficiency to meet every need with a divine surplus.

I see myself sharing this bounty for the good of all according to the guidance of Spirit.

I happily see every bill paid, and joyfully see every obligation met.

With great delight, I see the abundance continuing to flow to me. I am a divine magnet for money, and as I lovingly receive it, I lovingly use it with great wisdom.

ELEVEN

The Angels and Physical Healing

Based on the Principle of Wholeness, we are complete and perfect in both the invisible and visible. Our mind is as pure as its source, and our body is flawless and unimpaired at every moment of our journey on the third-dimensional plane—for there is nothing but perfection throughout the infinite universe.

This is the Truth of our being, and if our physical system seems to say otherwise, it is because we are believing a lie. It is this "virus in the computer" that the Angel of Truth and Enlightenment loves to find and eradicate. False beliefs and error patterns dissolve when the sun shines on them, as ice melts on a summer's day. And as this melting occurs, we see a return to wholeness in the body. All twenty-two angels play a role in the healing process, but first we must free them, and then give them permission to heal our mind and emotions.

The unchaining begins with our willingness to accept the Law of Perfection as a personal and present reality, even though the idea may seem preposterous because of the way we look and feel. The liberation continues as we understand that we are not *in* the physical body, but rather the physical body is an element within each individualized energy field, existing as a mental concept in consciousness appearing as energy-in-form. When we grasp the significance of this, it dawns on us that we are not subject to the body, that we are not under its authority, and that it cannot dictate to us how we live. And the servant becomes the master.

Is the physical body real? Yes, because it is energy in configuration appearing as a body. Is it perfect? Yes, as the energy of the spiritual body manifesting as form—but it is made imperfect in our experience to the degree of imperfection held in consciousness. As consciousness realizes its perfect wholeness as the Mind of God in expression, so will the body, because the body is subjective to mind.

Let's remember that just as our Divine Self created the spiritual body through its imaging of the perfect Whole, so each aspect of that body is a divine idea united as one complete expression. As this energy-body is lowered in vibration, it appears as solid, or substantial.

How do we heal the body? We can't, because, as I said, the body is already perfect. When we know that—or awaken to that Truth—the perfection that already is is revealed, which brings us back to our mental–emotional system—our consciousness—the only thing that requires healing.

In *Esoteric Healing*, by Alice A. Bailey, we read that "in the subjective and hidden attitudes of the mind and of the emotional nature . . . must be sought the causes of all disease."[1] And "disease is therefore the working out into manifestation of undesirable, subjective conditions. . . ."[2]

This healing of the mind and emotions of hidden attitudes and undesirable conditions is not just modern metaphysics. It's ancient wisdom dating back thousands of years. In the old records are a number of reports of Masters healing their students by an act of energy transference to "cast out" the negative force. The biblical accounts of commanding evil spirits to leave a person—through the power of the Creative Word, the Pluto archetype—were based on a similar process.

As time progressed, the techniques evolved into a true science of healing, based primarily on realizing the Principle of Wholeness and the Reality of Self. *Realization* means understanding. When we truly understand who and what we are, all beliefs to the contrary are dissolved and wholeness is revealed in the physical system.

Frequently this dawning of understanding brings forth what we call a "miracle"—a supernatural happening—but miracles are nothing more than the marvels of the natural order of things. When we get back into the rhythm of the universe, we will find everything joined together in perfect balance, which is the meaning of the word *harmony*.

One of the best examples of what happens when we tune into this natural order was reported in the booklet "The True Stories of Today's Miracles," which was sent to subscribers of *Guideposts*.[3] According to one story, a bedridden woman was diagnosed as having a terminal disease, the doctor having told her that nothing could be done. A few years later the doctors confirmed that she was dying, but the woman didn't give up. She said, "The less physical health I had, the more I yearned for spiritual health." She prayed, talked to God, and became totally dedicated to achieving a healthy mind.

Then one morning she woke up feeling good about herself—"mentally, emotionally, and spiritually." That afternoon, in the company of two friends, she heard an audible voice over her left shoulder. It said, "My child, get up and walk!" She told her friends who had not heard the voice that God had spoken to her, and she asked that they summon her family. She then removed the oxygen tube and jumped out of bed and danced. When the doctor examined her later, he found no signs of the disease.

Can you see *consciousness* at work here? The absence of the disease was revealed after the woman had embarked on a dedicated program to heal the mind and emotions and release the natural flow of spiritual energy.

Within each one of us the threads of consciousness—based on our life experiences—are woven differently. The patterns buried in the subconscious vary greatly, yet there is no pattern or belief system more powerful than

God. The question, then, is how to access the power and come into alignment with the energy flow. There are as many techniques and formulas as there are people searching for a healing, and whatever works, works. Here are a few reports, beginning with one of my own.

Several months after her heart attack and near-death experience, Jan began to have a tightness in her chest and other symptoms of a heart problem. We were both concerned. I went into meditation, and the Angel of Truth and Enlightenment gave me two things to do: (1) prepare a statement of Truth for both of us to work on, primarily because I was having difficulty rising up into the pure, healing consciousness of the master Mind, and (2) ask a dear friend, Walter Starcke, to meditate with us. I followed both instructions.

The statement I wrote included these points, which we immediately took into consciousness:

Thoughts of impurity once held in mind, but now in the deeper recesses of consciousness, continue to influence the body and serve to support the idea that "I am not worthy to be free, therefore my life must be restricted . . . I cannot do what I really want to do because I am guilty and must be punished." There is no unforgiveness in the Mind of God, only in self. Forgive self and the thoughts of impurity are dissolved. No one can condemn self but self; no one can restrict self but self. Praise and free self and flow with Spirit in the river of life.

Say, "I cannot be punished for anything that I did or believed in the past, and this knowledge cancels out any such belief.

"Spirit sees my body as perfect; therefore, it is. I see with Spirit and recognize that God alone is the reality of my body.

"As of this moment, I am no longer blocked, restricted, withheld, inhibited, limited, curbed, bridled, constrained, curtailed, or bound. I flow easily with the life force flowing through me and I am free, unrepressed, unshackled, uninhibited, dauntless, bold, confident, and audacious. I can now be Me, as the inner flow cannot be interrupted and my heart beats in unison with the great Heart of the Universe. I am at peace within and without."

I also called Walter. He came to the house and meditated with us, and within hours all discomfort was gone. The three of us continued to work together for several days, and Jan has never felt better. Thank you, angels; thank you, Walter!

In another case of angel assistance, Yvonne in Canada wrote that her entire scalp broke out "with a million boils." Her doctor gave her antibiotics, which didn't help, and she was referred to a dermatologist, who said that it was a condition she would have to live with. Yvonne could not accept that verdict and went home to make contact with the Angel of Illusion and Reality. As she tells it:

Then I understood that rage and anger were what was causing these sores. Rage and anger from what? This is truly baffling. Then the Angel of Illusion and Reality impressed upon me to write a letter to my head. I called on this angel and the Angel of Victory and Triumph to help me write the letter. Excerpts from the letter are as follows:

"I understand that you have been aching and hurting and agonizing for a few centuries, but the time has come to let go of all of these negative emotions. You are so angry at the injustice of life and the unacceptance of your ideas, but what is, is. So what if others are not understanding or accepting of your beliefs, thoughts, and ideas. There is no need to be angry and no need to feel alone. You are only as different as you make yourself to be; but in truth, there is only one great Omnipotent God, the Father, Protector, and Provider—the Mother, Nurturer, and Lover—expressing through each of us. Therefore, even if your ideas are not accepted, you have been privileged to know Truth. Know it and let it be. The time very clearly has come to yield to the Presence of the God-Self and let God be everything through you. Release and let go of all rage, anger, resentment, injustice, hatred, bigotry, and low self-esteem. Let us cast all of this upon the Fire of Love."

I read the letter twice to my head, and the next day it started to feel better. Then two days later the Angel of Illusion and Reality began to work with my chakras, helping me to release the illusions held in each center, and I felt a healing. The angel said, "Now you have found a new joy!" And with those words the Angel of Order and Harmony entered. She told me, "Let your light shine and extend this light and joy to all those who share your world."

All the boils are drying up. All is well in my world. The light of God is all there is . . . isn't life wonderful?

Several weeks after receiving the above correspondence, another letter from Yvonne came in the mail with a healing meditation given to her by the Angel of Illusion and Reality.

> *The Light of God now fills my body.*
> *The Light of God now fills my soul.*
> *The Light of God now fills my being.*
> *The Light of God now makes me whole.*
>   *I am the Light which fills my body.*
> *I am the Light which is the soul.*
> *I am the Light which is this being.*
> *I am the Light and I am whole.*
>   *I Am the Light!*
>   *I Am the Light!*
>   *I Am the Light!*
>   *I AM!*

Meanwhile, in Philadelphia, Elizabeth was visiting the Angel of Truth and Enlightenment about her arthritis.

I asked him to shine through me and eliminate everything in my objective awareness that denied my perfection. I held myself in the light of the Sun and felt the divine rays shining through me. I repeated this process several times during the day and recorded in my journal the changes that were taking place in consciousness. After three days the pain went away and has not returned.

Mary in Los Angeles felt that her eye problems were due to the lack of "inner vision" and too great a focus she had placed on what was wrong in her life. She wrote:

I have found that the angels like to work together, so I solicited the help of two of them, the Angel of Illusion and Reality and the Angel of Imagination and Liberation. I asked them to assist me with my power of concentration and to focus my mind on all the things that are good in my life. They were very helpful, but it took me several weeks before I could dismiss unpleasant thoughts that came into my mind and refocus on the good. I'm getting better at it now, and it may be my imagination, but I think I am seeing better . . . I know I am in my left eye. I also know that when I can really feel that I am healed, I will be.

What prevents the feeling nature from pulsating with the energy of Truth is usually the reactive nature of the emotions telling us that we are not worthy to be healed because of past transgressions. In situations like this, we can make the correction in the emotional system through the heart center.

Whatever we impress upon the heart *with feeling* is transmitted to the emotional body, and that highly charged feeling immediately begins to transmute the old error patterns. First, we recognize and contemplate the infinite storehouse within—the kingdom that is already ours. The "good pleasure to give us the kingdom" is past tense. It was given as an extension of our Master Self, and the Self's focal point is the heart center. So we accept the truth that we have within us at this very moment the energy of all that we could possibly desire—in this case, the pattern of perfection for the physical body.

This radiant health and vitality are focused right in our heart center as energy. Make it a daily practice—ten minutes twice a day—to silently *feel* the energy of wholeness and well-being, reaching behind the words to discern the pulsating force, and letting that feeling harmonize your emotions. Remember that you are contemplating a divine attribute within, and not the physical system itself. This is important, because the emotional nature will not believe you if you say that your body is whole and perfect. It will consider that a lie because of the vibration from the old patterns.

This is a cooperative effort in working with Spirit. I have also used the following meditation to remove the illusion in consciousness and replace it with Reality—a Reality that will then express itself in the body.

> *God.*
> *God is.*
> *God is Infinite Mind, and I am forever in the Mind of*
> *God, the only place I can ever be.*
> *God is Life, and God's Life is my Life. I am an*
> *immortal Being, eternally expressing the Perfect Life of*
> *God.*
> *God is Unconditional Love, and that Love provides for*
> *me moment by moment, giving all and withholding nothing.*
> *God is Absolute Truth, the Reality of all that is, and*

*through the eyes of Truth, I see only Perfection in my
world.*

*God is Energy, the Cosmic Force and Power, creating
all that is out of the Energy of Itself. I am a pure
unadulterated Energy Field, individualized by God as God
in perfect expression.*

*God is Principle, the energized action of Mind as the
Law of Harmony in every activity of my life. I accept
this.*

*All that God is, I am. All that God has is mine. My
consciousness is whole, my body is perfect, and I am free.*

The energies of love, inspiration, and abundance can also be used to
transmute the emotions into true feelings of completeness. Edna in Dallas
had been working with the Angel of Unconditional Love and Freedom to
help with a chronic stomach problem. She had been told that the mental
causation was a lack of self-love. After several days of accepting love for
herself and others, the angel said:

*Why don't you accept the truth that I am you? I am your love nature,
the power of love that has always been within you. As love, you have the
power to heal. Be love, and you will rise from this infirmity.*

Edna wrote that she began practicing the idea that her identity was none
other than the Angel of Unconditional Love and Freedom, that the energy of
love was her whole essence, and that when anyone came within her pres-

ence, they would experience only love. She soon became so in tune with the love vibration that the stomach pain left her and has not returned.

In the ancient sacred academies it was taught that inspiration was the force to clear maya, the energy that would remove from the emotional body any justification for not achieving one's life goals. For example, we might feel that we can't accept a particular career opportunity, travel to another country, or become involved in a meaningful relationship because of a lingering physical malady. The malady is our maya, our excuse for not stepping out and fulfilling our dreams. The teaching said that when we can become truly inspired about life and live with inspiration, the maya is dissolved—in this case, the affliction.

Allen, a Boston resident, had attended one of our workshops in which we talked about this concept. Later he wrote:

I hadn't felt really good for a long time, always seeming to be in a state of fatigue and low energy. I've had tests run by doctors, but they couldn't find anything and I was getting even more depressed over my condition. Your talk about inspiration did motivate me to try it, but it didn't work—that is, until I met the Angel of Courage and Perseverance. He's been working with me to show me that I do have something to look forward to in life, and as the inspiration grows, the tiredness goes.

John in Cleveland wrote about the Angel of Abundance:

This lovely light-filled creature told me that the reason for my recurring back pain was because I had not been able to accept the truth that my Spirit was providing what was needed in the form of financial supply. The angel said, "You never think you're going to have enough, so you never feel prosperous. This feeling of being deprived is manifesting in your back, bending you over with fear. God has provided everything, and I am directing the energy of abundance directly through you into expression. Only you can block that expression. Nothing is withheld from you."

As I meditated daily on the message, not only did the pain go away, but I had a nice raise in salary.

For many of us, meditation is indeed the answer—a moving up into higher consciousness—but this form of meditation is not to heal, change, or improve something in the physical world. The intention is to experience the Presence of God. While in that Upper Room we contemplate the Wholeness, the Reality, the Perfection of our Holy Self, not praying or asking for anything, but focusing only on the light, the energy, the essence of that Infinite Mind.

The more we can forget our problems while in the meditative state, the greater the change will be when we come back into the phenomenal world. We discover that while we were communing with our Spirit, those precious angels within us, the twenty-two living energies, got together to produce a healing. But we didn't take any mental action to bring this about. We just went "up" to experience our Truth of Being, and what happened "below" was the natural action of the activity of God.

To me, healing of mind and emotions, thus revealing the natural wholeness of the body, is in direct relationship to our realization that we do not have a "human" nature. This has been the message of the Angel of Truth and Enlightenment since my first encounter with him. He continually emphasizes that everything seen and unseen is energy, *spiritual* energy, which means that it is real, and he has reminded me in so many ways that God is all there is, and that includes where we are and what we are. The sum total of all Energies expressed itself as the individualized Energy Field that we are, which means that there is nothing but God where we are.

The Truth Angel has said to me, to all of us:

Instead of trying to find out more about yourself, spend more time discerning the Truth about God. This is what "Know Thy Self" really means. As you know the Truth of God, it is the God-Self within knowing the Truth about Itself. When you speak the Word of God, it is the God-Self in you speaking the word, and nothing can stand in its way.

God-Self, your I AM, has never condemned Itself, so there is no condemnation in you. God-Self—I AM—has nothing to forgive Itself for, so there is no resentment in you or directed toward you.

God-Self, the I AM, is eternal Wholeness and maintains Itself from Its own Completeness, so there is nothing to heal.

The only Identity you have is God. There is no mortal

mind, for there is only one Mind; therefore, there is no "mind" to treat.

All that God-Self is, is in eternal manifestation of all that is good, so there is no duality to "demonstrate" over.

Omnipresence is; affirming does not make it so. Evil is not, so there is nothing to be taken away through denial.

There is no separation between you and God, for that would mean that there is something other than I AM. There is not.

The sense of separation is from the head, which has been sleeping. The Truth is from the heart, which is awake and is the throne of God-Self, the I AM.

Surrender to the heart, to Spirit, to Truth, giving to the one Reality that which you thought was personality. This surrender takes you into the Stream of Love, where your thought processes will be anchored. You will think from the heart, from feelings of love, and the head will awaken with spiritual illumination.

Not only will you feel and think Truth, you will also see it. You will look through spiritual eyes and see only that which is real in life.

Can you not hear God speaking to you now, asking that

you drop the idea of mortal self and let the Supreme Presence be the one Self?

Say yes, and look to the heart, and feel the love, light, and joy—the very Kingdom, Power, and Glory.

YES!

TWELVE

The Angels and

Relationships

One of the greatest resistance factors in consciousness—that which screens out the natural flow of good into our lives—falls under the heading of relationships. In my book *Empowerment*, I wrote: "Wherever there is any form of relationship, regardless of how casual or intense—whether with family, friends, associates in the workplace, even strangers—the law of cause and effect is in its most accelerated mode of action and reaction."[1]

That's because in most people, the Angel of Loving Relationships is practically smothered with ego projections. And until the angel is freed, we suffer more karmic repercussions through relationships than in any other activity of life.

Karmic causes did not come into play until the universe was thrown out of balance with the sense of separation—the dream of being separated from God and the formation of physical bodies. When the consciousness of unity and oneness of all life faded, the phenomenon of "relationships" came into being. The law of cause and effect became a part of the natural process at that time to restore universal equilibrium. It does this by bringing into balance through compensating factors every action for which we are responsible. On the outer scene we learn wisdom through experience; on the inner plane perfection continues because the law has thrown off the discord to be harmonized in the universal karmic process.

Just think about all the "sowing and reaping" that is done in interacting with others, particularly with those close to us. This is why the Angel of Loving Relationships is so vitally important in our lives. As we open ourselves to this Living Energy, it will guide us safely through the educative experiences of relationships, seeing that we learn the proper lessons for further consciousness expansion with minimum suffering. Sometimes the angel will use the past to help us prepare for the future.

A friend of mine living in Houston at the time sought greater understanding about her consciousness of relationships, particularly any hang-ups she might have that could sour a perfect union with a man. She was guided to ask the Angel of Loving Relationships to show her the relationship between her mother and father when she was a child. She wrote:

I saw my mother, very beautiful and young in her physical form, but full of fear and timidity, in love with my father but with many blockages from her past. She had very set ideas about how a marriage "should be" and how a family "should be." She was very insecure. My dad was very ambitious, hardworking, and almost fatherly toward her. She was his child more than an equal. He also had very set ideas and expectations about sex, money, and family values. There wasn't much spontaneity.

I saw myself as a little girl, full of life and love. I kept wanting to give to them, but the love kept bouncing off the blockages and back at me. I lost trust when I was rebuffed, when they couldn't share my joy. I realized my dad was afraid to love me . . . his fear of the sexual made him block love for me. So I got a fear of loving, and a fear of getting too close or intimate in relationships.

I was able to move beyond this in consciousness by beholding them in the Christ Light, seeing their True Nature, and sending healing to all of us. I also filled the house we lived in with light and love.

When this woman met a man at one of our workshops, love was soon in bloom. Later, as the relationship developed, she asked the angel if this man was her true soul mate. "Yes," cried the angel. The two are now happily married.

The Angel of Loving Relationships does a marvelous job of transmuting misqualified energy and eliminating any residue of fear, pain, and guilt from the past for the good of all concerned. Otherwise, a fear of relationships can quickly develop.

In her book *Loving Relationships*, Sondra Ray reveals that after her divorce, "I decided maybe I should avoid relationships. They seemed to be destroying me. And I noticed that many of my friends had decided the same thing. . . . My trouble was that I did not know how to use relationships for enlightenment and for healing myself. I didn't, quite frankly, know what was going on. Now I know no one can hurt me but myself. I know that if I feel hurt, there is something I have not cleared."[2]

That's one of this angel's primary functions: to help us clear up the emotional system and shift our consciousness into a higher frequency so that we can see a better way to handle our relationships. As Ray states it, "You and your partner can learn to get the maximum joy and value out of your relationship no matter how it turns out. You can even part and feel good about it. You can even get *exactly* what you desire in a relationship."[3]

When you make contact with this force of masculine and feminine energies, ask to be shown the key points in your relations with other people—your strengths and your weaknesses—and how the karmic boomerang, both positive and negative, has affected your life. Write this in your journal, along with a personal profile of how you wish to present yourself to others, the way you truly are: warm, loving, joyful, uplifting, interesting, nonjudgmental, and so on.

I went through this exercise once and was surprised when the angel said that I sometimes give the impression of being distant, detached, indifferent, and ready to run to the nearest hideaway to get away from people. I was told that in many situations, I put out an energy to keep others at a safe distance, saying in effect, "Do not get too close." The Angel of Discernment came in at this point and said to the relationship angel, "I've been working with him on this, because in the past he wasn't discerning at all and got burned a few times. Now he's carried it a little too far, but you and I together can get him into balance." I think they're succeeding. But I still get a bit flustered when I hear the angels talk about me as though I'm not there.

When the Angel of Loving Relationships is free, we may get the message that "the time is now—go for it." That's what happened to a woman in Dallas who's been very close to Jan and me. She wrote:

I was now ready for a permanent relationship in my life. I was really ready! . . . I decided in August that my intention was to be a radiating center of marriages made in Heaven—a marriage of unconditional love, joy, fearlessness, friendship, affection, partnership, incredible sex, spirituality, and prosperity. I tuned into this and radiated it out.

At the same time I saw my own wedding, right down to every last word that was to be uttered. I really got into it. Then I saw this all coming into my life, including different activities that were important to me that I wanted to share with someone. I gave thanks for my magnificent life!

Meanwhile, when any little blip came up about anyone or any situation, I remembered this, and I would send silent blessings to people everywhere to be in their own perfect relationship with someone who inspired them to be the best they could be. The more I did this, the more I realized that this was peace on earth, that if we were all with that one who really adored us, and it was mutual, peace would prevail. So it became my mission in life.

Well, "he" showed up at the end of October . . . and Cupid hit me with a giant arrow. Fortunately, he had already been hit and was just waiting for me to catch on.

The end of the story, and the new beginning, is that this beautiful soul and her man were married the following August.

Notice that this angel specializes in *loving* relationships, and the reason is that in its superconsciousness, only the highest form of bonding is seen with everyone. In *The Only Dance There Is*, Ram Dass writes that "an enlightened being is totally in love with the universe, in the sense that everything in the universe turns him on to that place in himself where he is love and consciousness."[4] This is what the angel is striving for: to turn us on to its energy, so that our consciousness radiates only love and goodwill to every soul we encounter.

Does this mean that we love the rapist or serial killer as we love a member of our family? From the universal standpoint the answer is yes, as we look past the appearance and recognize the God indwelling. While we may not like the personality, we can certainly love this "neighbor" as we do our Holy Self. This is important, because to despise another is to despise a part of ourselves, and we know how damaging that can be.

Think of a target with its various circles, with this impersonal, universal love for all as the outer circle. Let's move in now to the next circle and look at the wide range of our acquaintances. In this band of love, an encounter gives us the opportunity to silently salute the Holiness within the person, while expressing kindness, goodwill, respect, patience, and harmlessness toward the personality, regardless of what has previously taken place in the relationship. We must forgive in the larger circles if we're going to find fulfillment as we move in toward the center.

The next space in on our target is the family arena, our most difficult training ground. Prior to incarnation, we choose our parents and our children choose us, primarily for the lessons to be learned in working off karma from past lives. The compensation is usually satisfied by age twenty-one, and the only ties among family members at that time should be mutual love and respect, or the continuing of a close relationship based on the bonds of friendship that have been developed. For parents to hold on to their adult children is against the law of nature, and those offspring who live their lives primarily for their parents are compromising their spiritual integrity. Ralph Waldo Emerson put it quite succinctly in speaking to his family:

I must be myself. I cannot break myself any longer for you, or you. If you can love me for what I am, we shall be the happier. If you cannot, I will still seek to deserve that you should. I will not hide my tastes and aversions. I will so trust that what is deep is holy, that I will do strongly before the sun and moon whatever only rejoices me and the heart appoints. If you are noble, I will love you; if you are not, I will not hurt you and myself by hypocritical attentions. If you are true, but not in the same truth with me, cleave to your companions; I will seek my own. I do this not selfishly but humbly and truly. It is alike your interest, and mine, and all men's, however long we have dwelt in lies, to live in truth.[5]

In the next inner circle we find our friends, which may include certain members of our family, and the angel delights in uniting people in bonds of loving and lasting friendship. Kahlil Gibran said it all when he wrote, "Your friend is your needs answered. He is your field which you sow with love and reap with thanksgiving . . . you come to him with your hunger, and you seek him for peace. And let there be no purpose in friendship save the deepening of spirit."[6]

Our friends are those who accept us as we are. True friendship is a sharing relationship, a uniting in mutual understanding, where every opportunity is taken to contribute to each other's well-being. When a friendship is based on not what we can get but on what we can give, the karmic plates are positively etched with lasting compensation.

The next circle of love is our intimate, personal relationship where twin flames burn as one. There is a special ingredient that makes a significant difference in this love bond. It is *passion*. And oh, the Angel of Loving Relationships is indeed passionate! Passion in this context means deep feelings of love and ecstasy, fire in the heart, spirit, excitement, devotion. When we're with the right person, we feel this way not only about her or him, but also about life itself.

I've had the great fortune of being married for over forty years to a woman who exudes passion, and who has drawn it out in me to where everything in life is a glorious adventure. Perhaps the secret to our uniting as one is that we think of the other person's happiness first. Jan's joy becomes my joy and vice versa—and both of us love to play together and do things "just for the fun of it." Of course, it helps that we've been a team in many incarnations, so we've had plenty of time to get our acts together.

It's interesting that when my family moved to another town after my sophomore year in high school, our new home was only a couple of blocks from where Jan lived. I didn't pay much attention to her because she was going into eighth grade at the time and was "only a little kid." That perception was soon to change.

A few years later, I was in the U.S. Air Force stationed in Europe and Jan was in college in Texas. I had made plans to come home on a forty-day leave. One day my mother and aunt were eating in a restaurant in our hometown, and Jan stopped by their table to ask how I was. Mother told her that I would be home in a few weeks, and they exchanged pleasantries for a few minutes. As Jan was leaving, my mother turned to my aunt and asked, "Who is that girl?" My aunt replied, "That's Janis Bryant . . . she lives just down the street from you." And my mother said, "Something just told me she's the girl that John's going to marry." The Angel of Loving Relationships was beginning to set things up.

While home on leave, my mother gave an open house for me, and Jan came with some friends. When our eyes met across the crowded room, we knew that we'd found each other again. We dated every night, and on Christmas Eve I told her that I loved her. She said she loved me too. At the family Christmas dinner the next day I announced that Jan and I were going to be married—we didn't know when yet, but we were very much in love and wanted to spend the rest of our lives together. When I didn't get much of a reaction from the people around the table, I said, "Didn't anyone hear me?" And my mother said, "Oh, we already knew that. An angel told us."

In June 1953 Jan and I were married. We spent our honeymoon and our first year of marriage in Germany.

We embarked on our spiritual journey in 1967, and I know that this search for Truth together has deepened and intensified our passion for one another, for love and life, and for God. In the adventure of growing spiritually, we found that center circle of love—the "bull's-eye"—and the Truth that there is, indeed, only one relationship. That's the one with the Lord and Master Self within.

When we love that inner Essence, the very Spirit of God indwelling, then our whole world begins to change dramatically. J. Sig Paulson, an internationally known New Thought author and lecturer, has written that

> the first and great commandment is to love that inner
> Presence, that divine potential that is within each and every
> one of us. . . . As we do this, we become complete human
> beings. We begin to fulfill the laws of our own nature, and
> our method of expression changes. We stop identifying
> ourselves as just human beings, or weak human beings, or
> stupid human beings. We begin to identify ourselves as

spiritual beings, filled with the presence of God and
equipped with the divine potential of His Spirit.[7]

Imagine how that kind of identification can heal and harmonize a relationship. From this understanding of ourselves as spiritual beings comes the recognition of our powers—the energies of the angels—and we see that we are no longer bound to loneliness, frustration, and despair. That's when good things happen, including the excitement of serendipity.

Remember, from an earlier chapter, Elisha in Greece and her experience with the goat? Well, she flew over for a workshop we were having on the Guadalupe River Ranch, never expecting what was to come. As she tells the story:

I had allowed myself another week after the workshop to explore and relish the surrounding countryside. When a lady I had befriended at the ranch invited me to her hill country home, I once again thought how perfectly everything falls into place when I walk hand in hand with the angels.

I met many new friends in that week, and when they all insisted that I stay longer, I agreed. When my official permit of stay had come to an end three months later, I knew I had to stay on. I had only just begun to skim the surface of this gigantic continent's atmosphere.

"Do you really want to stay on?" asked the Angel of Materiality and Temptation. The question made me think. Money, paid work, accommodation, and transport were all uncertain propositions, and my return ticket was paid for and ready to take me back to my Mediterranean paradise,

where I was happily expected. Then a brightness from beyond the angel transcended and dissolved his image and I heard, "You are here to stay. You need to blend with the matrix of this continent in order to be fully useful as My Way. Trust. I am that I am."

I tore up my round-trip ticket, canceled it officially, and, since my visa was expiring, decided to leave the following morning for Mexico with the intention of returning to the U.S. after a while. One of my friends offered to drive me to the border, stopping first in town for a farewell tour of the shops. We finished up and got into the car to make our departure. As my friend put the key in the ignition, a white truck pulled up beside her.

"Hey, Robert," my friend called out the window. "Elisha's leaving, her visa is up. We're on our way to Mexico."

"Oh, no!" exclaimed Robert, with whom I had exchanged a few words some days earlier. He got out of the truck, came over to my window, and said, "Will you marry me?" My whole universe froze for an eternal moment. God, what's this? What shall I do? A totally loving, relaxed voice-vibration emerged from my inner depths and said, "Say yes to Life! Say yes to Me!"

I looked at Robert for a moment. "Are you serious?" I asked. And, "Are you marriageable? Do you have a sense of humor?"

To all three questions he answered with a swift "Yes!" Then I got out of the car, held out my hand to him, and said, "Yes!"

Now, more than two years later, both Robert and I can look back over our time together and laugh. The Angel of Unconditional Love and Free-

dom has taken its place of honor at the top of the table in my inner Crystal Hall, just as all the other angels are happily there in their rightful seats. Each one has given his or her support to me over these past two years, and I open my soul-arms wide for an all-embrace in deep gratitude.

Jan and I are grateful, too, that we have had the opportunity to be instruments for the angels in bringing people together, not only through our workshops but also through the written word. Doug in Michigan submitted an article for *The Quartus Report* on friendship and said that he would like to have a regular correspondence relationship with another Quartus member. We ran the article in the November 1993 issue, along with the plea for a corresponding friend. He soon heard from Kathleen in Utah. Doug says:

I then wrote Kathleen many letters and sent them on wings of love to her, and found quick response in a continuous flow back to me. My circumstances in Michigan continued to bring me blessed divine discontent, so the angels took me by the hand. I was first visited by the Angel of Renunciation and Regeneration, who suggested that I give up my old life and ways in favor of something new—to relinquish a life of outmoded and outgrown pseudo-paradise of denial. I was then guided across the country to Utah.

During the trip, much contemplation and inner searching found me wrapped in the spell of the Angel of Cycles and Solutions. In my travels, this angel took me into the deep valleys of wonder and doubt, preparing my consciousness for more effective solutions to the problems and opportunities for growth toward spiritual adulthood.

The Angel of Truth and Enlightenment met me at my destination and showed me what my former life contained: fear, doubt, low self-esteem, and anger. The angel then helped me to maintain my resolution to overcome former habits and to realize God's purpose in all things.

Finally, I was ready to listen to the counsel of the Angel of Loving Relationships, and on March 25, 1994, Kathleen and I were married. This new relationship has presented me with one golden opportunity after another to realize a fuller life of positive and serene beingness, and Kathleen has proved to be the very example I was to follow toward that true life of self-realization.

If you have an unceasing longing for a life partner, it is because you have something special to give to someone—that which the other person is seeking and wants very much. He or she also has a rare gift for you, a quality that will make you feel complete. But in order to give and receive specifically what is needed in each life, the two of you must find each other. The Angel of Loving Relationships is ready and waiting to help you find that missing person.

Today I send love to this world, and I call everyone my friend regardless of who they are or what they have done, for I see only the Spirit of God in every person, including myself.

I love the Completeness I AM, the Selfhood of God we all share as our eternal Reality. I look within to this magnificent Self and I say, I love you with all my heart, with all my soul, with all my mind, with all my strength.

And I love all my neighbors on Earth as I love my Self, for we are one.

I love unconditionally. I give my love freely, and that love returns to me in bountiful measure. I am worthy of love, of being loved, and I accept the love of others.

I think of all the people I know by name, and I feel the harmlessness and harmony that exists between us.

I look at my family unit, and I see only the expression of love, goodwill, kindness, and respect among all members.

I am thankful for my friends, and I see our relationships deepening in love, joy, and mutual understanding.

And I know there is a special Someone with overflowing love to share, who right at this moment is being attracted to the love I have to give, two flames soon uniting as one in a bond of love and ecstasy.

Love is everything. Oh how I love Love.

THIRTEEN

Angel Appearances and Other Strange Events

The universe is a field of pure energy, and our world is nothing but energy in manifestation. The angels are centers of Living Energy, and while they are anchored in twenty-two sectors within our individualized auric field, they are not confined to those coordinates. As we have seen in some of the angel experiences, they have the ability to express themselves and appear as another form—as a solid object, a figure of light with discernible features, or even as a physical body.

When an angel projects its energy and appears as a part of our phenomenal world, it is doing so within our consciousness, and it is our consciousness that is interpreting what we see based on the frequency that we are holding in mind. The form gives an appearance because our minds arrest the energy vibration—the whirling, dancing atoms—which enables the physical eyes to see those things we consider substantial and "real." The form may also be seen by others through the avenue of the collective mind.

For example, Jan and I once interviewed a woman regarding her remarkable healing powers. Later this woman told me that she wanted to do some work on my etheric body to release some trauma from a past life. This sounded ridiculous to me and I said, "I don't want to do that." As every part of me was resisting, I literally saw the Statue of Liberty walk through the door—not an apparition, not a mind's eye image, but a solid form as real as the room in which she was standing.

The woman said, "What does she mean to you?"

I was startled and said, "You mean, you can see her too?"

"Of course," the woman replied matter-of-factly. "Now, answer my question. What does she mean to you?"

"Liberty and freedom."

"That's what you're going to get if you sit down and shut up."

I did, and had an amazing experience of going back to the moment of death in another lifetime.

Who/what appeared as the animated statue? The Angel of Unconditional Love and Freedom, who knew that my health in years to come would be much better if that emotional shock from centuries before could be healed. And what better way to get my attention? The symbolism was perfect.

––––––

Another manifestation of ideal symbolism happened when my mother and stepfather were driving late one night on a deserted highway. My stepfather was doing about 80 miles an hour, and hadn't seen any lights behind him, when suddenly a huge black hearse appeared in the next lane, then passed them and immediately disappeared from sight. My stepfather said, "I wonder where that thing came from, and where did it go?" My mother said, "I don't know, but I think you ought to slow down."

Good advice, because as they came up over the next hill, a car without any lights was stalled in their lane. My stepfather was able to swerve and miss it, but only because of the appearance of the black hearse just moments before.

When Jan and I were called and invited to conduct our first workshop back in 1982 in Huntington, New York, we accepted, but with a certain amount of anxiety. *The Superbeings* had just been published, and we were concerned about talking to a large audience on the subject of Truth when we had not fully embodied the principles ourselves. We should have known better. It was a totally responsive and enthusiastic group. The prepared notes were quickly dispensed with, and we heard ourselves saying things that we couldn't have possibly known with our rational minds. Then we discovered the reason for this.

At the break on Saturday afternoon, a man asked me about the Chinese man and older woman who were standing behind us on the platform giving us information. I thought he was hallucinating and turned to walk away. Then a woman from another part of the audience came up and asked the same question. When we asked her to describe what she saw, she said, "An Oriental man dressed in a green-and-gold robe and an old woman in a white robe, both very physical in appearance."

A few months later, in Florida, it happened again. While signing books after the seminar, a young man whispered in my ear, "You know, you have people with you from the other side who are helping you and Jan in your presentation." When I asked what he saw, he described the same two people that were seen in New York, right down to the colors of their robes.

As the new kids on the block, so to speak, we had help from the angels that transmitted ageless wisdom, enabling us to reach those early audiences in a way that would not have been possible with our level of consciousness. They probably became visible to others so that their appearance could be relayed to us, thus negating any spiritual pride over our newfound ability to convey Truth ideas. We were not in this alone; we had holy helpers.

When only one person in a group has the visual experience, it means that the vibratory rate of the energy-as-form is relating solely to the specialized nerve endings of that person's particular sense organs.

For example, Michael and two of his business associates received a message at the Boston airport from their corporate office. They were told to fly to Chicago instead of Atlanta because of a change in plans for a conference. As they approached the airline ticket counter to purchase the new tickets, a man walked up and said to Michael, "Don't take the eleven o'clock plane. It's going to sit on the runway with mechanical problems, the flight will eventually be canceled, and you'll miss your meeting." This man gave Michael the name of another airline and said, "There's a plane leaving in twenty minutes. You can make it."

Michael turned to his coworkers and said, "Maybe this guy has inside information. Shall we try to catch the other plane?" They just stared at him. They had not seen or heard the stranger, and when Michael turned to question the man, he wasn't there. An angel in disguise? That's what Michael thought, and he and his coworkers were on board the other flight when it left a few minutes later.

When Jerry was hiking in the woods of Georgia, he encountered what seemed to be a "physical angel with wings." He wrote:

It seemed to float down and settle at the base of a large tree. I could hardly believe my eyes, and I was too much in awe to say anything. It was the figure of a woman, with long golden hair and a brilliant light all around her—but she looked very real and was even dressed in modern clothes, a long dress. It was the wings, though, that held me spellbound. And her voice was so beautiful . . . she said she came to tell me of rising floodwaters ahead and for me to turn back. I knew that for the first time in my life, I had really seen an angel.

Manly Hall has written that "the Rosicrucians and the Illuminati, describing the angels . . . declared that they resembled small suns, being centers of radiant energy surrounded by streamers of Vrilic force. From these outpouring streamers of force is derived the popular belief that angels have wings."[1]

We also have several third-person reports of a man or a woman suddenly appearing in the passenger seat of cars. While the occurrences were not witnessed by the people who told us the stories, in each case it was reported that the driver did not experience shock or apprehension. There was simply an acceptance that an angel had appeared in physical form to warn of approaching danger, to offer advice about a troubling aspect of life, or to answer an important question.

Eleanor in New York didn't see the angel in her car, but she did feel a distinct physical presence touch her.

My son, Andy, who had been diagnosed and treated for childhood acute leukemia and who had been in steady remission for seven years, developed a cough. It was persistent for a week, followed by a low-grade fever and lethargy. I began to worry . . . that this was the cancer recurring.

After about two weeks, I couldn't put it off any longer and scheduled a doctor's appointment for a blood review. On the way to my job on the day of the doctor's appointment, I was mentally wrestling with God, trying to exercise faith, trying to say "Thy will be done," and breaking down in tears. I was so upset that I began to veer off the road. When this happened a second time, I felt someone in the backseat lean against my right shoulder. I whipped my head around to see who it was and heard the most indescribable melodic voice (male). It said with a deep chuckle, as if there were some hilarious joke being told, "Eleanor, it's not THAT!"

After I had ascertained there really wasn't a visible person in the backseat, I pulled off the road because I was engulfed with joy and relief. I had instant and utter belief—the word had been spoken! I began to laugh so hard that my body shook. I sparkled my way through the day at my job . . . life was so funny! What a joke! It wasn't "THAT"!

The doctor's appointment, which I had almost canceled, turned out to be a confirmation that Andy was probably catching the measles, and that his spots would probably appear in a day or two. More whoops of laughter, then giggles, when true to form, the spots appeared. When they left, the fever and cough left too.

Simon in Nashville also told of a physical presence of an angel, as reported by his girlfriend at the time. He wrote:

All through our relationship I had shared my spiritual beliefs and awareness with her. She was fascinated with my stories of guardian angels, helpers, and guides, but she was content to let me do the spiritual exploring.

When I had to go to Kentucky for a couple of weeks, she found herself missing me and very lonely. She told me when I returned that one night she couldn't sleep and was lying in bed on the verge of tears. Abandonment was one of her issues, and on that night it was getting the better of her. She said she began talking to her angel, "just as though there was really someone there." As she talked about her loneliness and the tears began to flow, she said she noticed that something about the room changed. She continued to talk, and then, very gently, a hand took hold of her hand. The hand that held hers felt warm and soothing to her. She felt love flowing through her hand and filling her with an overwhelming sense of peace. Before she could express her wonder and gratitude, she fell asleep.

A few nights later, as she talked to her angel in the night, the same thing happened again. Her face lit up with the excitement of new awareness as she told me of the reassuring touch of her angel. She said she realized that, even when she was by herself, she was never really alone.

Angels can also appear in a crowded restaurant, as told by a woman living in the Midwest.

I can remember one time when an angel appeared to me. At the time I thought it was just a person who could magically read my thoughts.

Several years ago I was in the midst of a very troubling situation at work. I felt no support from peers during a bad time with my supervisors, and was completely demoralized and probably depressed in a clinical definition of the term. I was having suicidal thoughts and was not able to even fathom the idea of other options—killing myself seemed to be the only way out from my deep sadness.

Well, I was sitting in a restaurant one afternoon, just staring off into

space after giving my order, when a woman, a stranger, slid into the seat op-
posite me in my booth. She looked me straight in the eye and said, "Do not
commit suicide." She talked to me a little while longer, and I don't remem-
ber the exact words, just that the words were along this same line. I was
speechless. I just nodded agreement, then she left. I never gave another
thought to suicide. The situation at work did not improve, but I was not so
demoralized by it. I eventually left the job and found work where I would
say to myself at least once everyday—"So this is what happiness feels like."

Enid in Missouri shared this story:

Shortly after my mother made her transition, I was meditating with my
prayer group. I felt a sense of completion with the meditation and was wait-
ing for the others to stir. Suddenly before me was a shimmering, vibrating,
cloudlike essence of lavender, pink, and silvery light. It floated in a wavelike
manner before my eyes and was sort of upright in form, tapering near the
bottom.

I instantly thought, "Oh, an angel!" I had never seen an angel before
and I was excited. My second thought was, "No, it's the Divine Mother!"
Tears began to flow down my cheeks because of the intense love and joy I
felt. I was overwhelmed.

As the others in my prayer group began to stir, a friend sitting next to
me said, "Enid, you must have had a wonderful experience."

I said, "Oh, I did! I was visited by an angel that I finally decided was the
Divine Mother."

And she said, "Or your mother." She went on to tell me that my mother was there with us and had given her a message for me. The personal message was such that I knew no one could have given it but my own mother.

An angel? The Divine Mother? My own mother? All? I was blessed beyond measure by all three!

Other people who have written to us about their encounters with angels have described these beings variously as a large luminous light; a mighty flame suspended in midair; a huge angel, about twenty-two feet tall, with enormous wings, thick brown hair, and wearing a long robe; the shape of a physical body, but made of pure light; someone who looked to be a gardener; a young boy, about age ten or twelve; a kindly gentleman with white hair and a beard; a beautiful young woman in a flowing white dress; an old woman, very ancient; a Native American; a black woman; a cowboy on a white horse; a Samurai warrior; and an old friend.

In *The Many Faces of Angels*, Harvey Humann writes:

> For many centuries, angels have graced us with their
> presence. . . . It is little wonder they are so indelibly fixed in
> our collective minds as enduring archetypal figures. They
> conjure up a thousand images and meanings for both
> believers and unbelievers. For believers they are a living
> mystical part of everyday life who console, inspire, guide
> and protect, and for unbelievers, a brilliant adjunct to our
> religious culture.[2]

I am willing to accept unexpected, unusual, and astonishing happenings in my life, for I am not fearful of that which comes from God by way of the angels.

There is but one Presence in this universe, and I am one with that Presence. There is but one Power, and that Power is good, loving, and benevolent. Knowing this, I step out in faith, ready to experience that which has been hidden to minds closed to the extraordinary.

I now open myself to the incredible wonders of life, to new adventures that contribute to a greater understanding of the mysteries of the cosmos.

I seek to believe the impossible, to witness strange and wonderful events, to behold phenomena that elude reasonable explanation. I am prepared to hear the inner voices of angels, to see the visible demonstrations of their hidden hands, and to accept their sudden appearance before me in physical form.

Angels, I choose to see, hear, feel, and know the multiple realities of other dimensions. Standing in God's Love and Light, I am ready. Let the experience begin.

FOURTEEN

Dialogues with the Angels

Talking to yourself can be a favorite pastime. When combined with controlled imagination, the exercise can be quite fruitful in lifting consciousness and opening the channels of communication. Most people may not understand the mystical importance of such action. I know that I didn't, until I began having in-depth conversations with the angels.

It all started one morning following meditation. I was thinking about an article that I was scheduled to write, but I couldn't seem to get the right thought energy flowing. So I called a conference of the twenty-two angels and asked if one of them would volunteer to have a dialogue with me to open my mind to greater understanding on a particular topic.

You can do this, too, and receive information on essentially any subject or question you have in mind. I encourage you to establish dialogues with one or more of the angels even before you finish this book, and using a tape recorder is an excellent way to do this. You'll find that the angels enjoy playing the role of teacher and broadening your base of knowledge, if you carefully follow their instructions.

To continue, when all the angels were gathered on this particular morning, I asked for ideas on discussing the causal power in our lives. The Angel of Power and Authority stood up and said, *"I'll be glad to help, but I will not say anything that will go beyond the possibility of your comprehension, for that would be fearful to you at this stage of your development."*

"Why is that?" I asked.

He replied, *"Concepts that threaten your present belief system—ideas that you may not fully understand—cause shock waves in your emotional body and so are screened out, diluted if you will, when you attempt to present them to others. Frankly speaking, you are fearful of not knowing what you're talking about."*

"Then how am I going to learn more and grow in spiritual understanding?"

"Through meditation on the Presence of God within, which opens and expands consciousness to receive the sacred truths, and through our spoon-feeding of ideas into your objective mind to slowly melt down old beliefs and construct new ones."

"Will discussions with the angels on particular subjects speed up that process?" I asked.

"*Definitely. Such an exchange with us will provide a learning experience for you, and will certainly contribute to your understanding—provided that you first still the mind and emotions and through imagination move into a question-and-answer mode with our energies. And be sure to interpret and express the words that come through according to the frequency of your consciousness.*"

"What do you mean?"

"*Don't make us sound archaic. We'll be using your thought patterns, your language, so don't translate as a more refined transmission. Also, use your imaging faculties to see us interacting with you during the dialogues. That will provide greater clarity in the communications.*"

"I understand. Well, shall we give it a try?"

The Angel of Power and Authority replied, "*I'm ready whenever you are.*"

Dialogue One—With the Angel of Power and Authority

I opened the discussion:

"Let's start with the concept of Cause, the power behind all effects, in a way that can contribute to general understanding."

The Angel of Power and Authority said, "*All right, but first I want to tell you about implosion. Do you know what that means?*"

"Implosion means bursting inward, kind of like the external suddenly crashing in on the internal."

"Do you realize that you have described how ninety percent of the people of this world live? Just think about how many times you have heard people talk about what has happened to them, or what they anticipate happening in the future. It's as if there is something out there hiding in the shadows that jumps out every so often to deprive or debilitate them. Listen to people: They talk about getting some disease, the possibility of being fired from their jobs, fear of not having enough money for their old age, what the husband-wife-children are doing to them, how the political or economic conditions affect them.

"Everything is OUT THERE, a conspiracy to rain on their parade and remove the joy and happiness from their lives. They are living with past implosions and waiting for more to happen."

I said, "I guess that's human nature."

The angel looked at me in a kind, gentle way and said, *"Most people live under the laws of the third-dimensional plane, and the common principle of that body of laws is a belief in averages; thus life is lived on the continual role of the dice. Humans appropriately call this playing the law of averages, and every instinct is sharpened for the game—for both the losses and gains. They live as though the world of effect ruled their lives, as though something 'out there' had permanent dominion over them without recourse, or that 'something' was a force to be attacked, fought, and eventually conquered by the power of God."*

"Is it time for questions?" I asked.

Ignoring me, the angel continued. *"Most of the people you know have a fear of something, but did you ever stop to consider that the only basis of fear is belief? So people only fear their beliefs and nothing else, and beliefs can be changed. People must find their point of contact within and anchor their minds and emotions to that aspect of reality. When they do, they will begin to understand that there is no power in the phenomenal world that can affect them, unless they identify with it as a power and accept its authority."*

The angel then suggested that we go outside. As we did, he seemed to take a deep breath and turned away from me for a moment. When he turned to face me, I could almost see fire in his eyes.

"Look up at the sun," he commanded.

I had to lean back and look almost straight up to see it.

He said, *"The sun does not worry about deprivation, scarcity, disorders, or afflictions. It doesn't care about anything but being itself and eternally sharing all that it is. It knows that it is a law unto itself, and it lives as that law—and the same principle holds true for you and everyone else. Understand this: Every soul is a point of universal power. Focus on that word: point. Think of it as a tiny dot of light within your consciousness. That point is the aperture through which all-that-God-is flows, radiates. It is the expression of your Self, your Divine Consciousness, and it is the absolute law and perfect cause of everything in your experience—controlling the interior workings of your body and fanning out in extended streams of radiant energy to reach and touch everything registered by your senses in the outer world. Everything out there is a manifestation radiating from that point of light, and YOU are that point of light, as is everyone else."*

"Then, in a sense, we are all 'exploders' rather than imploders, because all action is from within out."

"Yes! Each individual is the cause and the law of his or her life. You are literally pressing out into existence all that you experience, and once you begin to live as the inlet and the outlet for that Divine Expression, you will never have another threat to your harmony and happiness."

"I noticed that you said, 'live as.' "

"That is the secret. At every moment you must live as cause, live as 'I am the cause and the law to my world.' Remember that the outer scene is nothing more than the lines of force emanating from within and made visible without. Say, 'I am the molder, maker, controller, and creator of my affairs, of every experience of my life.' Say it now with power."

"I am the molder, maker, controller, and creator of my affairs, of every experience of my life!"

"I AM is the point of light. I AM is the point of power. I AM is the point of creative activity. I AM is the cause. I AM is the law. I AM is YOU! You are the light of the world, your world. A light shines, it radiates, flows, projects. That beam of light extending from you paints all the pictures on the screen of your life. It triggers every experience, manifests every form, expresses every condition, arranges every circumstance.

"You are the only law and cause in your life. This means that nothing in

the phenomenal world can cause suffering, sorrow, lack, conflict, accidents, failure, or danger because there is no power outside of you. There is no cause or law external to you. You are the great cosmic molder and your world is putty in your hands."

I asked, "Where does an individual start in putting his or her world back into shape? You said earlier that our only fears are our beliefs, so I guess we begin by changing our belief system."

The angel said, "*You begin by changing your identity. Performing surgery on the subjective level can be a long and tedious process, so why not rise above the old error patterns? The personality believes; the Divine Self KNOWS. When you identify yourself with your Self and live in that identification, the radiation of your Divine Consciousness passes over the lower beliefs, and they soon wither and die of their own accord.*

"*People simply have to cease playing the role of the human. It's not something they were trained for, you know, and that's why they make such a mess of their parts.*"

"Maybe we should stop being actors and start being producers and directors," I said.

The angel looked at me for a moment without speaking. Then he continued: "*Did you hear what you just said? Perhaps this discussion hasn't been in vain after all. Actors train themselves to create illusions in a show that is being produced and directed by others, and doesn't that describe the plight of most humans? As you learn to move from personality, which wears the actor's mask, and up into the realm of Soul, you become the director of your affairs and the producer of your activities. You take on your true identity and become the Law of Right Relations, the Law of Supply, the Law of Health, the Law of Success, the Law of All Good in your life. Right at this moment you are the Shining Sun of God. Can you not look within and see the source of that shining?"*

I said, "With the inner eye I can perceive the light, and I feel its radiation. It's beginning to resemble a searchlight, and I can see the beam extending out into my world. I see now that I am that searchlight!"

The Angel of Power and Authority smiled and said, *"Hold that understanding in your consciousness and know that your good is not something to come from the world of form, nor do you ever again have to make something happen. All that you could possibly desire is contained in the radiance, and it is now moving from cause into effect through your awareness. This is the meaning of the statement in the Bible that says, 'Solomon made an end of praying . . . and the glory of the Lord filled the house.' "*

Dialogue Two—With the Angel of Order and Harmony

It was now well past midnight and I was sitting on the back deck of our home and looking at the stars. I felt that the Angel of Order and Harmony wanted to participate in a dialogue, so I called her into my conscious awareness, a beautiful young woman in a robe of golden light. After our greeting, I asked, "What does 'heaven on earth' really mean?"

She answered my question with a question: *"What is your definition of heaven?"*

"In this context I guess I would define it as harmony."

"And what does harmony mean to you?"

I thought for a moment. "It comes from a Greek word meaning 'to fit together,' so it means having everything and everyone joined together in one accord—compatible, in agreement, in unity and balance. To live in harmony is to live without conflict, contention, or hostility."

The angel said, *"That is the state of livingness of the Soul-Self. And 'heaven on earth' is simply the descent of the energies of the Higher Aspect into the lower, where the Divine Self assumes authority over the personality."*

She stood up and began to slowly pace about. *"I want to tell you why the kingdom has not appeared in the lives of many people, including those considered truth seekers. There are basically three reasons: a misunderstanding of the will of God, a tendency toward self-denial, and a victim consciousness."*

She seemed to wait for my comment. "Go on," I said.

"Let's take the will of God first, as perceived by many disciples on the spiritual path. They practice blind acceptance of their circumstances because they feel it is God's will, and one excuse frequently used for this acquiescence is that karmic debts are being repaid and there is no escape from the conditions. My question is, how long do they think retribution continues? Karma is but the law of cause and effect, and any action producing adverse circumstances can be neutralized by right action.

"*Errors producing like-manner consequences can be transformed into freedom from the negative effect through the same law, and the transformation is essentially immediate. Each individual controls his or her own destiny, and to blame difficulties in life on God's retribution is a travesty.*

"*Tell people to replace the spirit of submission with the spirit of fight, and to go into the world to capture and secure beachheads of happiness and joy. Forget the past with its self-imposed limitations. People do not have to 'bear' anything but life, and life is magnificent, sumptuous, and grand for those who escape from the idiotic cage of their own construction.*"

Listening to the angel speak, I remembered that the Romans considered this archetype, which they called Minerva, the goddess of war, because order can only be achieved through the destruction of that which is in disorder. I was about to comment on this when she said, "*You yourself have experienced comfort zones of restricted living which you accepted as part of the lessons of life. You have experienced the effect of a negative use of the law presented as a lesson, but any schoolchild knows that you do not live with the lesson forever. Once you've seen what you have done, the lesson is over, and you dispense with it by realizing that you do not have to accept disharmony.*"

"We break the chains of blind acceptance," I said. "Now, what about self-denial?"

The angel asked, "*Do you use affirmations?*"

"Of course."

"*They can be very helpful if used properly. If not, they can cause a block in consciousness, thus preventing the emergence of the kingdom. Suppose a body appears ill, or a bank account seems insufficient, and the person is told to affirm his way out of the problem with the idea that he is in truth divine, and nothing divine can experience sickness or lack. While this idea is factual, the method is questionable.*

"Autosuggestion is a form of self-hypnosis, which only masks the problem and allows the person a method of escape by pretending the problem is only imaginary and does not exist. In the process, not only is the law of cause and effect denied, but also a part of the self. Subjectively, the person feels that if he is innately divine, then the other phase of his mind must be the opposite—sinful and evil. Rather than accepting and approving of his whole self, he begins to live in a negative state, denying everything except his unrealized divinity. And soon the predominant characteristic in consciousness is futility."

"So what's the answer?" I asked.

"Look at a problem for what it is—an opportunity for correction. The most priceless gift of God is an individual's free will, which means that each person can choose his own destiny. That includes the power to eliminate problems by facing the adversary squarely and slaying it. You do this by putting your whole self into the battle—the physical, emotional, mental, and spiritual you."

"What about the idea of letting go and letting God?"

"That teaching has also been misinterpreted," the angel said. *"To let go and let God means that your Holy Self will do the work, but only as you*

consciously represent that Self in the world. You know that Spirit works through a mind of one accord—not through a weak and helpless state of consciousness. Same thing applies to 'I of myself can do nothing.' To interpret this correctly is to say that the personality alone does not have the power, but when connected with the Divine Self, there is nothing you cannot do.

"The point of this discussion on self-denial is to show you that ALL of you is divine, so love, honor, and glorify the whole you while the Self is reaching out to take control and awaken the lower nature."

I asked, "What about the victim consciousness?"

"All three problem areas tie together. In your philosophy of life, the student is taught that everything that happens to him is a result of his own error thinking, that he has created his own undesirable conditions; thus he is a victim of his own consciousness. That is a heavy load to carry, one that can block out the kingdom for many on the path. Yes, consciousness does express itself, and that law is your passport into heaven as you learn to work with it. The lower consciousness is nothing more than a child playing with the power of God, and the experiments can sometimes go awry. But you learn by doing, not by sitting in a cave of safety. And if you make a mistake on your journey, that doesn't make you a victim.

"Tell people to take a chance, to LIVE—to not be afraid to risk it all—to throw their whole being into life and enjoy every moment of it."

I said, "I just remembered that the root meaning of *victim* is animal sacrifice. When we all begin to understand that our will is our free use of God's will, and when we stop sacrificing ourselves through self-denial, we might just wake up one fine morning and find ourselves living in heaven on earth."

The Angel of Order and Harmony looked up at the starry sky and said softly, *"Why wait until morning?"*

Dialogue Three—With the Angel of Materiality and Temptation

I had been in discussion with the Angel of Materiality and Temptation earlier on the idea of "grounding," and I was walking the fence line on our property when I heard him ask, *"The new year will be here in a few days . . . are you ready?"*

"Yes," I replied, "with great anticipation. It's like a fresh snowfall without any tracks, or a new book with twelve chapters to be written."

"Who is going to make the tracks in your snow and write the living scenarios in your book? Before you answer, look back over the past year. How many footprints were made by others playing out your projections, and how many of the pages in your book of life did you actually pen from a consciousness of mastery?"

I felt the noose getting a little tight and said sheepishly, "Okay, I get your point. I'll admit that there were days that seemed to be scripted by some outside force, days with an undercurrent of concern, periods of blahs, even times of sadness."

We walked over near the fence and sat down on an old log. The angel said, "*On those less than positive days, you simply relinquished your authority to maintain control over the channel you are. You slipped back into the illusionary dream, forgetting momentarily that you have the power to stay focused on reality. And in your living slumber, or weakened mental state, you let something 'out there' affect your mood, and thus your life.*"

"I know you're right," I said, "but it's so difficult to always be in control of mind and emotions."

The angel gave me an understanding smile. "*Well, let's not fret over what was. Hardly anyone is exempt from worry, and those in physical incarnation are particularly vulnerable to seasons of anxiety. To those close to you, there is an underlying concern of what could happen, rather than what has been. And people in the spiritual light are naturally more sensitive to the planetary situation and are touched in some degree by the suffering of others. But contrary to popular opinion, nothing positive can be accomplished by worry. In fact, worry is one of the primary causes of every type of difficulty on this planet.*"

"Aren't you stretching the point?" I asked.

"*Not really. The worry energy, which rises up from the emotional nature, impairs the immune system, directly affects the respiratory system, weakens the power and authority center at the throat, reduces the ability to see from the higher vision, and attracts the energy of disorder, confusion, phobias, and futility.*"

"Good grief!"

"Grief, yes, but not so good."

I said, "There must be a practical way to break the grip on worry and get on with the business of living."

That knowing smile came on the angel's face. *"Have you forgotten my name?"* he asked.

"It's Janus. The month of January was named for you, and people used to pray to you when they were starting something new."

"Then you know that January is the ideal month to take on the anti-worry energy and cleanse the emotional system of worry stains from the past."

Nodding as if I knew, I asked, "Okay, how do we do that?"

"By cooperating with my energy, the same energy that was used to initiate students in the old secret schools. The master representing Janus wore a mask showing two faces, one looking forward and the other backward. The latter was to look behind to make certain that the door to the past was closed. This involved an exercise in purification, and the practice is carried on even today, particularly on December 31, with people writing down everything they want to leave behind before they enter the door to the new year—and then they burn the paper.

"The Janus energy, which is another way of referring to my force of dynamic spiritual aspiration, is the power that dissolves the old and prepares one for the opportunities ahead. I do this by implanting a higher spiritual vibration in consciousness."

"And that's where the forward-looking mask comes in," I said.

"*Correct,*" the angel said. "*By focusing on the energy of spiritual aspiration, you will be lifted above the worry stream. Once you feel your oneness with the energy, you must work with it throughout the month of January. This establishes the foundation for the rest of the year, particularly if you will also meditate daily on these ideas.*"

The Angel of Materiality and Temptation then gave me these statements to use:

> *I release all attachments to the physical plane, break the chains that have bound me, and I look UP.*
>
> *I seek only the Holy One within, and I am drawn to the High Peak where all spiritual qualities unite in the magnetic fire.*
>
> *Initated in the light of understanding, love, and mental clarity, the way of the Plan now unfolds before me.*
>
> *I will not be complacent, for I am motivated to make life's journey a highly creative experience.*
>
> *I am devoted to the balancing of will, power, intelligence, love, and wisdom in every activity of my life.*
>
> *I have found the peace divine wrapped in the calm of wisdom. I am detached from the restless noise of the emotions.*
>
> *I breathe the thin airs of the pure mental plane, and active intelligence is the vibration of my mind.*

I embody the dynamic will and power divine, the thrust of all creation.

I carry the torch of truth, casting the liberating light on the climbing path.

I am protected and guided along the rocky heights, untouched except by the gentle hand of Love.

I am lifted by the strong hand of Love as I ascend the Holy Mountain.

I am fearless and strong, and I leap the chasm with ease and grace.

Power and knowledge flow into my heart as I move toward the Sunlit Peak.

I see the spiritual essence within all forms, and I create structures within the forms.

I am dedicated to organization and order, and I thrill to the harmony of joyous discipline.

I welcome transformation and change in my life, for I know that my Soul's purpose is unfolding.

I am one with Thought Divine, one with God in absolute Bliss.

The angel then said, *"These words are keyed to the Janus energy, my ray of spiritual aspiration. By incorporating these ideas in consciousness, you will be cooperating with a force that is the very antithesis of worry and concern."*

He was right.

Dialogue Four—With the Angel of Abundance

The month was November, and I was thinking about another new year approaching. Because of some seeming financial restrictions, I had been talking to the Angel of Abundance, the Venus energy. She told me where the circuit was crossed in consciousness, then asked me if I was ready for the new year. I casually nodded, not really wanting to think about it.

The angel said, *"Perhaps nakedness is the secret of preparation."*

I looked at her lovely form and figure, the dark hair falling on her shoulders. *"Nakedness?"*

"To be naked is to be uncovered, exposed. It is to return to unembellished simplicity, to essentials without the ornaments and frills of pride and pity."

I wondered to myself. Do we dare expose ourselves to others and let them see our warts of vanity and the marks of our lamentations? I may not be who I appear to be, and neither are other people. I thought about the symbolism: In my closet are coats of hidden dreams, supercilious shirts, trousers of futility, and shoes that seem too large for comfort in walking toward the sun.

As I stepped back to get a better look at this wardrobe, I heard the angel say, *"Either add to what you have, or clean it all out and begin anew."*

I said, "That's tough. Why can't I just replace certain items, rather than add or subtract?"

"Because it doesn't work that way," she said.

After a deep sigh, I said, "But I don't want to give up everything. If I empty the closet, I'll have to go to all the trouble of disposing of the old and accumulating the new."

"Just clean out the closet, and throw on the heap what you're wearing at the present moment, beginning with the shoes. And don't worry about accumulating anything."

"I would be totally bare."

She grinned. *"That's the idea."*

"How long would I have to stay in this stripped state?"

"Until you let me select the wardrobe," she said.

"What do I do first?"

"Confession is good for the soul."

"Oh, no. This is getting ridiculous."

"Not really. Just sit back and tell me in great detail about those secret fantasies, the unfulfilled aspirations, the regrets, where you feel especially prideful, and your areas of futility. Think of me as an understanding friend who never judges, never raises an eyebrow, and certainly never condemns or lectures. Come on, let it all come out."

Much later . . .

"*Now, that wasn't so bad, was it?*" the angel asked.

I said, "Good Lord! I've never told anyone some of that stuff. I really got down to the nitty gritty, didn't I?"

"*Feel better?*"

"Absolutely!"

"*Now, let me explain something,*" she said. "*Everything you told me is nothing more than a desire to taste life in all of its fullness—a longing to experience the excitement and adventure of living on the far edge as you lightly dance on the rainbow. Nothing wrong with that.*

"*Understand the symbolism of the reveries. They are all representations of deeper yearnings that can now be fulfilled because you have brought them into the light. And those blemishes you spoke of, they can now be removed because you consented to expose yourself.*"

"You wouldn't have a fig leaf handy, would you?" I asked.

The angel laughed. "*Forget it. That old story about the opening of eyes and being afraid because they were naked was what started that silly sin business in the first place. No, instead of leaves to cover up something, let's get you some tailor-made clothes to reveal fulfillment, contentment, and the realization of your dreams. The new year is almost here, and you'll want to take advantage of that window of opportunity.*"

"How do I do that?"

"*By knowing that all that could possibly be manifest in the phenomenal world as form or experience is within you, regardless of how incredible or outlandish such an expression might seem to you. It's all there now! So stop looking outside of yourself for anything. Got it?"*

"Got it."

"Also, any attribute that you require for a more meaningful life on earth is within you too. All the love, intelligence, wisdom, peace, power, understanding . . .

I interrupted. "But what about . . ."

"Be quiet and listen. You want money? Your spirit knows that you require money to operate efficiently in the world of form and takes great pleasure in providing, through me, all that is needed, with plenty left over. You want to help people? The Presence knows how to do that in the most creative way. You want to write a great book to break through the crust of the collective mind? That spirit of you can write world-class books. And those personal and private dreams, awake and sleeping? The consummation is waiting only for you to provide the channel for their perfect expression. Regardless of what you or anyone else wants in life, the fulfillment is already fully present. Do you hear what I'm saying?"

I nodded.

"Then quit trying to create something in the outer that has already been created in the inner. Just let that which IS flow. The fountain of abundance, creativity, wholeness, relationships, success, service, and everything else in life cannot be turned off. So go inside to the fountain, to your spirit, and drink!"

I was trying to be humorous when I asked, "What about my new clothes?"

The angel said *"You don't get those until midnight on New Year's Eve."*

"What am I supposed to do in the meantime?"

"Stay focused in your mind," she instructed. *"As your awareness of the Presence within deepens, your shoes will fit, your pants will be creased with worthiness and value, and your shirt will be stitched with true humility. Your tie will be striped with powerful intentions, and your coat will be a magnificent blazer of wildest dreams come true."*

"I can't hardly wait," I said, and meant it.

"Then don't," the Angel of Abundance said. *"Happy New Year."*

The Living Spirit within me is God as me, as my only Reality. I feel the love, life, and infinite knowingness of this indwelling perfection now—above, below, around, and through me.

I look within, and with the inner eye I see the Light of the Holy Presence radiating from the center of my being. It is the shining Light of Spirit, and as this Divine Brilliance streams into my consciousness, it diversifies into a spectrum of twenty-two living energies. These are the angels of my soul, the messengers of Spirit to lead, guide, and instruct me.

They are here with me now, and I have but to ask, and I shall receive. I understand that each angel has its own area of specialization, so I formulate my questions and call forth the appropriate messenger, always knowing that the right one will appear for the matter of discussion. I do this now.

I ask and I listen. Intuitively, the answer comes. I relax and silently speak again, and the dialogue begins. I feel the words echoing through my mind, and then with the inner ear, I hear the sweet voice speaking to me from within. The communication line is open, and I record the transmission in my journal.

I speak. I listen. I write.

FIFTEEN

An Angel Looks to the Future

In *The Divine Love and Wisdom,* Emanuel Swedenborg, the eighteenth-century religious mystic, wrote about receiving an answer to a very complex question from the angels: "It has been disclosed to me by angels, to whom it was revealed by the Lord; and because they had made it a part of their wisdom, and it is the joy of their wisdom to communicate to others what they know, permission having been granted, they presented before my eyes. . . ."[1]

The angels had presented him with the answer to his question, not only in words but also in visual pictures. Their wisdom comes from the Lord-Self within, and they will joyfully share that loving intelligence with us when we ask—if such information is beneficial to our spiritual growth ("permission having been granted").

On one occasion, when I was doing research for another book, I called an angel conference and asked about the future of our world. The reply from the Angel of Death and Rebirth was, *"The future is not fixed, for it is predicated on the consciousness of the race, and consciousness can be changed."*

I said, "But what about planetary cycles, those cosmic and biological rhythms that affect our minds and influence the collective consciousness? Each one of you represents a magnetic force, an astrological energy that affects human nature. Is there any particular cycle coming up that will have a dramatic effect on world events?"

There was only silence, and the picture of the angels on the screen of my mind went blank. I waited several minutes for the image to return, but no visual impressions came forth, neither were any words spoken from within.

A few days later, following meditation, I was aware that the Angel of Patience and Acceptance had slipped into my stream of consciousness, and I greeted this "Queen of Heaven" warmly. She initiated the conversation by saying, *"Understand the energy of reconciliation that is coming forth—a cycle of spiritual intelligence, moderation, and acceptance."* Perhaps permission had been granted, and over the next thirty to forty minutes we talked about the intense magnetic radiation that would impact the earth beginning in 1995.

Archetypally, we were discussing the energy of fundamental upheaval uniting with the energy of spiritual regeneration. In its symbolic portrayal, it is judgment interacting with temperance, and, astrologically speaking, it is the cycle that occurs every two hundred or so years when Pluto, the power of dramatic change, enters Sagittarius, the force of idealism and direction.

The angel said, *"The universal aspects of this energy will shape consciousness to have a sense of proportion in life, to dispense with fanaticism and an overly aggressive devotion to a cause or teacher in the phenomenal world, and to place emphasis on the receiving of spiritual truth from within. The result will be dramatic changes in religion throughout the world, for this is the cycle of the white horse."*

I asked, "When you say 'dramatic changes,' I'm assuming that you are speaking from a positive point of view. What do you mean by 'the cycle of the white horse'?"

She said, *"A new fellowship of religion will eventually come forth in recognition of the inherent truth and beauty of all faiths, but in the interim, there will be an uprise of rigid religious intolerance throughout the world—and beliefs will be severly tested. In time, fear will give way to understanding, and fanaticism will be replaced, first by indifference, and later by a willingness to let people worship in peace according to their own consciousness.*

"Shortly after the turn of the century, a new sense of religious freedom will move across the land, and regardless of religious beliefs, individuals will be accepted on their own merits as members of the planetary family, and the idea of unity through diversity will be universally acknowledged.

"The white horse I am referring to is the one in Revelations 6:1–2."

A quick look at that chapter and verse in the Bible revealed: "Now I saw when the Lamb opened one of the seven seals, and I heard one of the four living creatures say, as with a voice of thunder, 'Come!' And I saw, and behold, a white horse, and its rider had a bow; and a crown was given to him, and he went out conquering and to conquer."

In *Alter Your Life*, Emmet Fox writes:

> The White Horse is the Spiritual Nature, and the man or
> woman who rides the White Horse gets freedom, and joy, and
> ultimate happiness and harmony; because the White Horse is
> the realization of the Presence of God. When you put God first
> in your life, when you refuse to limit God, when you will no
> longer say that God cannot do something, when you trust
> God with your whole heart, you are riding the white horse,
> and it is only a question of time until you shall be free—when
> the day will break and the shadows flee away."[2]

Curious as to the astrological implications of the white horse cycle, I found two articles by professional writer and astrologer Alex Miller-Mignone in *Planet Earth* magazine. He writes: "Pluto in Sagittarius will . . . signal the revival of fundamentalism to a degree unprecedented in modern history, with disturbing ramifications globally for humanity's evolutionary unfoldment."[3]

Miller-Mignone also says that when the cycle is complete,

> the tide should have turned in favor of these new energies
> permeating the collective. The basic principles of the
> Aquarian Age, stressing respect for the individual within the
> needs of the collective, each person's connection with
> divinity superseding arbitrarily imposed rules of conduct,
> and the responsibility of each individual in the creation of
> his or her own reality, will have gained a permanent
> advantage over the old paradigms of disempowerment and
> fear.[4]

I continued my research on this cycle of change, wondering if there were
any predictions of conflict, and whether or not the upheaval would bring us
closer to a new world religion. In Alice Bailey's writings I found the Tibetan
master Djwhal Khul urging all religions to eliminate mutual antagonisms,
otherwise "humanity is headed toward a religious war which will make the
last war appear like child's play."[5]

Djwhal Khul also said:

> The day is dawning when all religions will be regarded as
> emanating from one great spiritual source; all will be seen as
> unitedly providing the one root out of which the universal
> world religion will inevitably emerge. . . . They will accept

the same truths, not as theological concepts, but as essential to spiritual living; they will stand together on the same platform of brotherhood and of human relations; they will recognize divine sonship and will seek unitedly to cooperate with the divine Plan. . . ."[6]

Seeking to understand more fully the dramatic upheavals we may be facing, I called on the Angel of the Creative Word, the Pluto archetype. All he would tell me was, *"Look back at history."*

I did, and had to go back to the mid-1700s to find the last time this particular cycle of energies made its appearance. According to *Webster's Guide to American History*, the religious revivals that had spread from New England to the southern colonies began to be "resisted for different reasons by both conservatives ('Old Side') and liberal ('New Side'). . . . All Protestant sects are affected, various conflicts and schisms arise."[7]

In America and Europe, these new energies also resulted in the blossoming of the Age of Enlightenment and laid the foundation for the intellectual revolution that followed. An upswing in deism, the religion of reason, made a profound impact on such minds as Benjamin Franklin, Thomas Jefferson, Thomas Paine, and Alexander Pope. Pope, the English poet, had said he could no longer pray to the traditional God, but must now address his prayers to the "great First Cause."[8]

This shift in thinking from a supernatural to a "natural" religion based on universal laws caused a sharp decline in orthodox religious belief among the middle and upper classes. It was also reported that "all the churches— Catholic and Protestant—suffered a severe loss of prestige. Even the Catholic kings of France, Spain, and Austria, though they remained loyal to the faith, weakened the power of the Church by allowing no interference from Rome in the conduct of their affairs. . . . Most significantly, they forced the pope to dissolve the Jesuit order, which had achieved an arrogant power in Catholic countries."[9]

As the angel had indicated, whenever we have the force of upheaval combined with the energy of spiritual intelligence, we can expect dramatic changes. But, as the Angel of Patience and Acceptance told me later, *"In the previous cycle, the consciousness of the people was not ready for a complete spiritual revolution. New forms of democracy had not yet been birthed, and the people needed to experience a greater sense of individual freedom to further develop their intuitive nature, open their imagination, and probe the unknown and the mystical."*

She was right. We first had to have the Declaration of Independence and the Bill of Rights, Thomas Paine's *The Rights of Man*, the anarchy of Thoreau, the self-reliance of Emerson, and the rebirth of ancient wisdom. Now we are ready for the new reformation.

It is also interesting to look at the previous Pluto-in-Sagittarius cycles and see the heightened awareness and dramatic influence of angels. In the cycle of 1256 to 1270, Thomas Aquinas, considered one of the greatest Christian theologians, wrote *Summa Theologica*, and angels were immediately the talk of the church. The book "contains a whole treatise on the angels, as well as additional questions on the speech of angels, their hierarchies and orders, the division between the good and the bad angels, and their action on men. . . ."[10]

In the next cycle of religious change, 1502 to 1516, John Calvin was born. He became one of the foremost leaders of the Protestant Reformation. While angels became a favorite topic for him after the cycle had concluded, it is obvious from Calvin's writings that the energies strongly influenced his awareness of these "messengers of God."

In the cycle of 1748 to 1762, the resurgence of angels was extraordinary. Famous philosophers, historians, poets, statesmen, and theologians wrote extensively about angels, and the mind aggregate became conditioned once again to their presence. The key figures of this period were Bishop George Berkeley, Anglican bishop and philosopher; Edward Gibbon; Goethe; Kant; Herman Melville; Emanuel Swedenborg; and Voltaire.

"The polytheist and the philosopher, the Greek and the barbarian," wrote Gibbon, "were alike accustomed to conceive a long succession, an infinite chain of angels . . . issuing from the throne of light."[11] His emphasis was on historical references to angels.

Berkeley and Kant wrote about "suprahuman persons," while Goethe's primary topic was the will and love of angels, Melville's the guardianship of angels, and Swedenborg's their love and wisdom. Voltaire's primary contribution was "Angels," in *A Philosophical Dictionary*.

While angels have been the subject of many books, television shows, and movies in our time, I feel that during the new cycle of change that began in 1995, angels will become a distinct reality for more people than ever before. It may be a time of upheavals and convulsions in some areas as the old order disintegrates, but the angels will show us how to face change creatively and move through uncertain times with ease and grace. As *A Course in Miracles* reminds us, "You do not walk alone. God's angels hover near and all about."[12]

Men, women, and children of all religions throughout the world will find that they do indeed have a holy helper—a force to lift them up above the slings and arrows, a miracle-working power to be a very present help in trouble.

We know this. We have seen the evidence.

So perhaps the keynote of life should be the ancient admonition *KNOW THYSELF*. When we do, the Living Energies are freed, and we become what they are—strong helping hands, and a loving voice of comfort and support to all who cross our path.

When people exclaim, "You're truly an angel," we won't have to say a word.

We'll just know they speak the truth.

APPENDIX

Chart of the Angels

(For an in-depth discussion of each angel, refer to *The Angels Within Us.*)
The italicized questions indicate what the angel can do for you.

1. Angel of Unconditional Love and Freedom.

Has Unconditional Love replaced all judgment of people and conditions in your life, to where you are now free to live your highest Truth and let others do the same? This is the angel that sets you free to be your Self and to recognize that same Self in others. It is also the angel of the "awakening energy" and is known to work with the other twenty-one as the Eternal Power and Cause.

ARCHETYPE: Tao, Krishna, Master of Heaven, Spirit

PLANETARY ENERGY: Uranus

SYMBOLIC (TAROT): The Fool

2. Angel of Illusion and Reality.

Have you awakened spiritually in sufficient degree to see that which is false and that which is true in your world? This angel will make this clear to you so that you do not waste time in worrying about things that have no meaning or reality in your life.

ARCHETYPE: Hermes, Mercury

PLANETARY ENERGY: Mercury

SYMBOLIC (TAROT): The Magician

3. Angel of Creative Wisdom.

Is your intuitive nature illumined with the flow of Divine Wisdom and Inspiration? Known as "the keeper of the mysteries," this angel imparts spiritual wisdom and gives you the ability to solve problems quickly.

ARCHETYPE: Isis

PLANETARY ENERGY: Moon

SYMBOLIC (TAROT): The High Priestess

4. Angel of Abundance.

Are you living a bountiful life of prosperity, beauty, and well-being? Often called the all-nurturing Mother Goddess, this is the angel of substance and supply, embodying love, beauty, and power in constant expression.

ARCHETYPE: Venus, Aphrodite

PLANETARY ENERGY: Venus

SYMBOLIC (TAROT): The Empress

5. Angel of Power and Authority.

Is your life ruled by spiritual power and authority from within, where you live with great energy and strong decisiveness? This angel has been called "the Great King of the phenomenal world" and will help you follow the will of God in every situation.

ARCHETYPE: Osiris, Hercules, Jehovah

PLANETARY ENERGY: Aries

SYMBOLIC (TAROT): The Emperor.

6. Angel of Spiritual Understanding.

Do you have spiritual perception, and are you sufficiently open minded to receive deeper truths? This angel, also known as the "Master of Esoteric Knowledge," is the masculine counterpart of the Angel of Creative Wisdom.

ARCHETYPE: The Grand Master

PLANETARY ENERGY: Taurus

SYMBOLIC (TAROT): The High Priest

7. Angel of Loving Relationships.

Are you enjoying a loving relationship in which the duality is unified and you and your partner complete each other as one? This angel has the responsibility for insuring that you always make the correct choice in relationships and is the primary energy in courtship and marriage.

ARCHETYPE: Anubis

PLANETARY ENERGY: Gemini

SYMBOLIC (TAROT): The Lovers

8. Angel of Victory and Triumph.

Are you achieving your goals and fulfilling your life's purpose with a feeling of joyful accomplishment? The victory angel is the one responsible for helping you to meet your objectives with ease.

. ARCHETYPE: Serapis

PLANETARY ENERGY: Cancer

SYMBOLIC (TAROT): The Chariot

9. Angel of Order and Harmony.

Are you living a life of harmony and peace, with divine order in all your activities? This angel also maintains balance and fairness in situations and inspires you to live with honor and integrity.

ARCHETYPE: Athena, Minerva

PLANETARY ENERGY: Libra

SYMBOLIC (TAROT): Justice

10. Angel of Discernment.

Are you prudent and judicious in your thinking, always taking actions based on a proper understanding of the situation? This angel will train you to be a master of proper discrimination and keep you from making mistakes resulting from impetuous behavior.

ARCHETYPE: Adonis

PLANETARY ENERGY: Virgo

SYMBOLIC (TAROT): The Hermit

11. *Angel of Cycles and Solutions.*

Do you have the ability to accept change and move into new cycles of life with the attitude that nothing but good is taking place? This angel, which has been called the Energy of Miracles, will help you to face change creatively.

ARCHETYPE: Zeus, Jupiter

PLANETARY ENERGY: Jupiter

SYMBOLIC (TAROT): The Wheel of Fortune

12. *Angel of Spiritual Strength and Will.*

Do you have the mental will, emotional determination, and physical fortitude to follow the spiritual path, regardless of worldly temptations? This angel will help you to answer this question in the affirmative and will supply you with the power and conviction to move purposely toward the Light.

ARCHETYPE: Daughter of the Flaming Sword

PLANETARY ENERGY: Leo

SYMBOLIC (TAROT): Strength

13. Angel of Renunciation and Regeneration.

Have you surrendered your emotional attachments to the effects of the material world, thus freeing you to move into the Kingdom Consciousness? This angel will show you how to have nothing on one level in order to possess everything on another. It is the energy of abandonment and gain.

ARCHETYPE: Poseidon, Neptune

PLANETARY ENERGY: Neptune

SYMBOLIC (TAROT): The Hanged Man

14. Angel of Death and Rebirth.

Have you gone through the metamorphosis of crossing out the ego and realizing your identity as a spiritual being? You can be lifted into Cosmic Consciousness through the energy of this angel. It is also known as "the one who brings blessings in disguise."

ARCHETYPE: Thanatos, Death

PLANETARY ENERGY: Scorpio

SYMBOLIC (TAROT): Death

15. Angel of Patience and Acceptance.

Are you able to trust the divine process with total acceptance of "come what may," living each day with calm equanimity? This angel also imparts the energy of moderation and the ability to compromise when it is for the greater good.

ARCHETYPE: Iris, Queen of Heaven

PLANETARY ENERGY: Sagittarius

SYMBOLIC (TAROT): Temperance

16. Angel of Materiality and Temptation.

Are you strong enough spiritually to be suddenly awakened from the dream state and find yourself in the light of the fourth dimension? An instant leap into Cosmic Consciousness without adequate preparation could throw your energy field out of balance and set you back even further in the natural reawakening process. This angel helps you to stay grounded until you are spiritually ready to awaken.

ARCHETYPE: Janus, the Tempter

PLANETARY ENERGY: Capricorn

SYMBOLIC (TAROT): Old Pan

17. Angel of Courage and Perseverance.

Regardless of what is going on around you, are you able to see, think, and speak only spiritual truth? Sometimes it is difficult not to judge appearances, particularly when adversity seems to strike someone close to us. This angel provides the energy of steadfastness and the courage to live the Truth of our being.

ARCHETYPE: Ares, Mars

PLANETARY ENERGY: Mars

SYMBOLIC (TAROT): The Tower

18. Angel of Service and Synthesis.

Are you motivated to greater service to the world, and is your faith focused only on that which is good in life? This angel will help you to understand why service is a primary requisite for receiving the energy of the Master Self.

ARCHETYPE: Ganymede

PLANETARY ENERGY: Aquarius

SYMBOLIC (TAROT): The Star

19. Angel of Imagination and Liberation.

In the light of your imagination, can you see the reality of heaven on earth, a world of love, joy, peace, and freedom? This angel gives you the spiritual sight, the vision of the Holy Self within, enabling you to see that which can be and that which already is in the Higher Mind.

ARCHETYPE: Artemis, Diana

PLANETARY ENERGY: Pisces

SYMBOLIC (TAROT): The Moon

20. Angel of Truth and Enlightenment.

Has your lower mind yielded control to your Higher Nature, so that you are now living daily in that divine vibration? This angel possesses the energy of the transcendental consciousness, and also distributes the healing energy from the etheric into the physical system.

ARCHETYPE: Apollo, Ra

PLANETARY ENERGY: Sun

SYMBOLIC (TAROT): The Sun

21. Angel of the Creative Word.

Are you spiritually empowered to speak the Word to dissolve conflicts in your life and to create new conditions according to the divine standard? This angel enables you to rise above the third-dimensional effects into the realm of Cause, where all matters can be effectively settled for the good of all.

ARCHETYPE: Hades, Pluto, Phoenix

PLANETARY ENERGY: Pluto

SYMBOLIC (TAROT): The Judgment

22. Angel of Success.

Are you in your true place, doing what you love and loving what you do? This angel provides the energy to be truly successful in the material world through self-knowledge and a consciousness of oneness with all people and things. It is the energy of dominion.

ARCHETYPE: Kronos, Saturn

PLANETARY ENERGY: Saturn

SYMBOLIC (TAROT): The World

Notes

Introduction

1. John Randolph Price, *The Angels Within Us* (New York: Fawcett Columbine/Ballantine, 1993).

2. John Randolph Price, *The Superbeings* (New York: Fawcett Crest/ Ballantine, 1988).

3. Manly P. Hall, *The Secret Teachings of All Ages* (Los Angeles: Philosophical Research Society, 1977), 58.

4. Edwin C. Steinbrecher, *The Inner Guide to Meditation* (Wellingborough, England: Aquarian Press, 1982), 29.

5. *Biblical Encyclopedia*, "Angel" (Cleveland, Ohio; New York: The World Publishing Co.).

6. Charles Fillmore, *Mysteries of John* (Lee's Summit, Mo.: Unity School of Christianity, 1946), 68.

7. *A Course in Miracles*, vol. 1 (Tiburon, CA: Foundation for Inner Peace, 1975), 109.

8. *Holy Bible, Authorized King James Version, Condensed Bible Commentary*, "Holy Spirit" (Cleveland, Ohio: The Word).

9. Ernest Holmes, *The Science of Mind* (New York: Dodd, Mead, 1938), 480.

10. Fillmore, *Mysteries of John*, 136.

11. Alice A. Bailey, *Esoteric Astrology* (New York: Lucis, 1951), 244.

12. *A Course in Miracles*, vol. 3, 85.

One: The Mighty Hands of the Angels

1. Ralph Waldo Trine, *In Tune with the Infinite* (Indianapolis, Ind.: Bobbs-Merrill, 1947), 111.

2. John Randolph Price, *The Angels Within Us* (New York: Fawcett Columbine/Ballantine, 1993), 126–127.

3. John Randolph Price, *Practical Spirituality* (Boerne, Tex.: Quartus Books, 1985), 133.

Two: Inner Guidance from the Angels

1. Joseph Murphy, *The Amazing Laws of Cosmic Mind Power* (West Nyack, N.Y.: Parker, 1965), 77.

2. Ibid.

3. John Randolph Price, *Empowerment* (Boerne, Tex.: Quartus Books, 1992), 61–62.

Four: Divine Assistance Is Always with Us

1. John Randolph Price, *The Angels Within Us* (New York: Fawcett Columbine/Ballantine, 1993), 258.

2. Ibid, 259.

3. Ibid, 260.

Five: Communication with Angels in Dreams

1. Manly P. Hall, *Dream Symbolism* (Los Angeles: Philosophical Research Society, 1965), 4.

2. Joseph Campbell, with Bill Moyers *The Power of Myth* (New York: Doubleday, 1988), 39, 40.

3. Hugh Lynn Cayce, ed., *The Edgar Cayce Reader* (New York: Coronet Communications/Constellation International, 1969), 90.

4. Ibid, 92.

5. John Randolph Price, *Practical Spirituality* (Boerne, Tex.: Quartus Books, 1985), 127–130.

Six: The Angel Fire of Purification

1. John Randolph Price, *The Angels Within Us* (New York: Fawcett Columbine/Ballantine, 1993), 171.

2. G. R. S. Mead, *Fragments of a Faith Forgotten* (Hyde Park, N.Y.: University Books, n.d.), 500.

3. Newton Dillaway, ed., *The Gospel of Emerson* (Wakefield, Mass.: Montrose Press, 1949), 6.

Seven: The Angels Reveal the Truth

1. Alice A. Bailey, *The Labours of Hercules* (New York: Lucis, 1974), 94.

2. A. C. Bhaktivedanta Swami Prabhupada, trans., *Bhagavad-Gita as It Is* (New York: Bhaktivedanta Book Trust, 1968), 169, 173.

3. Manly P. Hall, *The Secret Teachings of All Ages* (Los Angeles: Philosophical Research Society, 1977), 40.

4. Newton Dillaway, ed., *The Gospel of Emerson* (Wakefield, Mass.: Montrose Press, 1949), 14.

5. Manly P. Hall, *The Phoenix* (Los Angeles: Hall, 1931), 51.

Eight: The Angels Are the Laws of Life

1. Alice A. Bailey, *The Rays and the Initiations* (New York: Lucis, 1960), 375.

2. John Randolph Price, *The Angels Within Us* (New York; Fawcett Columbine/Ballantine, 1993), 10.

3. Emmet Fox, *Alter Your Life* (New York: Harper & Row, 1931), 3–4.

4. Joel S. Goldsmith, *The Infinite Way* (San Gabriel, Calif.: Willing, 1947), 145–146.

Nine: The Angels and Right Livelihood

1. Charles Fillmore, *The Revealing Word* (Unity Village, Mo.: Unity School of Christianity, 1931), 187.

2. Ernest Holmes, *Creative Mind and Success* (New York: Dodd, Mead, 1957), 34–37.

Ten: The Angels and Prosperity

1. Newton Dillaway, ed., *The Gospel of Emerson* (Wakefield, Mass.: Montrose Press, 1949), 52, 54.

2. *Metaphysical Bible Dictionary* (Unity Village, Mo.: Unity School of Christianity, 1931), 620.

Eleven: The Angels and Physical Healing

1. Alice A. Bailey, *Esoteric Healing* (New York: Lucis, 1953), 9.

2. Ibid., 112.

3. Barbara Comminsky, "The Miracle Day," in *True Stories of Today's Miracles*, Harold Hostetler, ed. (Carmel, N.Y.: Guideposts Magazine), 13.

Twelve: The Angels and Relationships

1. John Randolph Price, *Empowerment* (Boerne, Tex.: Quartus Books, 1992), 79.

2. Sondra Ray, *Loving Relationships* (Millbrae, Calif.: Celestial Arts, 1980), 78.

3. Ibid.

4. Ram Dass, *The Only Dance There Is* (Garden City, N.Y.: Anchor Books/Doubleday, 1974), 60–61.

5. Newton Dillaway, *The Gospel of Emerson* (Wakefield, Mass.: Montrose Press, 1949), 50.

6. Kahlil Gibran, *The Beauty of Friendship* (Kansas City, Mo.: Hallmark Editions, 1978), 23.

7. J. Sig Paulson, *The Thirteen Commandments* (Lee's Summit, Mo.: Unity School of Christianity, 1964), 126, 127.

Thirteen: Angel Appearances and Other Strange Events

1. Manly P. Hall, *The Secret Teachings of All Ages* (Los Angeles: Philosophical Research Society, 1977), 51.

2. Harvey Humann, *The Many Faces of Angels* (Marina del Rey, Calif.: DeVorss, 1986), 65.

Fifteen: An Angel Looks to the Future

1. Emanuel Swedenborg, *The Divine Love and Wisdom* (New York: Swedenborg Foundation, 1949), 257.

2. Emmet Fox, *Alter Your Life* (New York: Harper & Row, 1931), 17.

3. Alex Miller-Mignone, "Pluto in Sagittarius Preview: You Ain't Seen Nothin' Yet," *Planet Earth* 13 (1994): 17.

4. Alex Miller-Mignone, "Pluto in Sagittarius: Question Your Paradigm," *Planet Earth* 14 (1994): 17.

5. Alice A. Bailey, *The Externalization of the Hierarchy* (New York: Lucis, 1957), 542.

6. Alice A. Bailey, *The Problems of Humanity* (New York: Lucis, 1964), 140.

7. Charles Van Doren and Robert McHenry, eds., *Webster's Guide to American History* (Springfield, Mass.: Merriam, 1971), 35.

8. George K. Anderson and Robert Warnock, *The World in Literature*, vol. 2 (Chicago: Scott, Foresman, 1951), 16.

9. Ibid.

10. William Gorman, ed., *The Great Ideas, A Synopticon of Great Books of the Western World*, vol. 1 (Chicago: Encyclopedia Britannica, 1952), 5.

11. Ibid., 3.

12. *A Course in Miracles*, vol. 2 (Tiburon, CA: Foundation for Inner Peace, 1975), 478.

About the Author

JOHN RANDOLPH PRICE is the author of more than a dozen books on esoteric philosophy and metaphysical principles and is the cofounder, with his wife, Jan, of the Quartus Foundation for Spiritual Research, Inc.

In recognition of their global peace efforts through the establishment of the Planetary Commission for World Healing, John and Jan were named the recipients of the Light of God Expressing Award by the Association of Unity Churches in 1986. In 1992 John was presented the Humanitarian Award for Peace by the Arizona chapter of the International New Thought Alliance, and in 1994 he received the INTA's Joseph Murphy Award in appreciation of his contributions to positive living throughout the world.

John can be reached through the Quartus Foundation, P.O. Box 1768, Boerne, Texas 78006.

Printed in the United States
37348LVS00006B/43-51